Vintage Dessert Recipes

Timeless and Memorable Old-Fashioned Sweet Recipes from Our Grandmothers

Louise Davidson

ISBN: 9781704720968

Printed in the United States

www.thecookbookpublisher.com

CONTENTS

INTRODUCTION

In this book, we've collected an assortment of dessert recipes ranging from as far back as the 1800s all the way up to the 1970s. Some are wholesome comfort foods, like potato doughnuts and pecan sticky buns, and others are kitschy and eclectic, like Green Angel Lime Cake and Orange Raisin Gems.

In my family's recipe boxes there were so many things we wanted to share, but we had to be selective. Some ingredients that used to be common, like suet, are no longer so easily available, and vegetable shortening is out of favor health-wise. We'll use the rule of "everything in moderation" when the shortening is necessary, and substitute butter or coconut oil where we can. However, we did want to be true to the original recipes, so we have not made wholesale adjustments – what you see here is almost all the original formulas. Luckily, most of the ingredients are still very common (and wholesome, if not exactly healthy).

We know you have a thousand recipes, so in this collection we've included foods you won't have – but we think you'll love them all. (None of our gelatin salads have grated carrots, we swear!) But we also wanted to tweak your memory a little, and hopefully bring to mind some things you know and love.

In this book you'll find recipes for pies, cakes, custards and puddings, cookies and bars, and loaves and muffins. No matter what the occasion is, there will be something here you can make and share. What's more comforting than a warm custard? Try the Raspberry Custard Kuchen. Need something portable and impressive? I'd recommend the Pistachio Cream Cheese Refrigerator Cookies!

In my last book, I talked about the connection we forge with our ancestors when we prepare the foods they ate. Since then, I've also been cooking more with my children, preparing some of these foods with them. It's fun to be able to say, "My grandmother made these very same cookies!" or "I remember a party my parents had when I was small. This is the gelatin salad someone brought, and I thought it was amazing."

Preparing the foods of our childhood brings back memories, and none better than those of sharing a delicious dessert with our loved ones. We can pass that feeling along! Try our Amish Applesauce Cake with some hot cocoa after skating, or take some Strawberry Kisses along on a picnic. A box of Oreos will not make the same kind of memory as a bright, sweet cookie your kids prepared with you.

Vintage Bakeware

If you love vintage things, as I do, you may be tempted to dig out some old cake pans or buy second-hand enamelware. Please be cautious – it is never safe to eat from a chipped or eroded pot, and many of the pie tins (and even crystal!) contain unsafe levels of lead. Also, as beautiful as copper cookware is, it's a heavy metal and can leech into your food. Copper on the outside of the pot is fine, but the inside should be stainless steel.

Distressed vintage enamelware is lovely, and when I see it I think of the people and kitchens it might remember and talk about, if it could. If you love it too, you can still have and use it – but in different ways. A pitcher can be a vase. A basin can be filled with ice and used as a cooler at your backyard barbecue. Bowls can hold fruit or napkins. You get the idea! Just don't cook in these charming old dishes.

Temperature Conversions

How much is a dollop? For some of these conversions we can guess: a dollop would be about two tablespoons, for instance. A dash is one shake.

Temperatures are a little harder to sort out. Many of these recipes came from when ovens were heated with wood, and these days we're more into actual temperatures. What is a "hot oven"? Here's a handy chart.

Description	Temperature
Cool oven	200°F
Slow oven	300 – 325°F
Moderate oven	350 – 375°F
Hot oven	400 – 425°F
Fast oven	450 – 500°F

Also for those more familiar with metric measurements, there is a handy Conversion table for both measuring and temperature equivalents at the end of book in the appendix.

Preserving Family Recipes

As you can probably imagine, when my grandmother passed away I was not the only adoring granddaughter she had. A few of us were eyeing those recipe boxes with their stained and fingerprinted cards filled back and front with her beautiful handwriting. My cousins and I also loved the little clippings from newspapers and magazines. We settled on an informal division, and said we'd sort it out later. Twenty years have passed, and we still haven't taken steps to preserve and share the cards. Here are some of the things we'll likely do, when we finally get around to it. It's important to us because we want to pass these along to our children.

Unfortunately, recipes were not written on acid-free cards, and the food, heat, steam, smoke, and general humidity of kitchens makes them a hostile environment for paper. Preserving them the way a library would preserve precious books is complex and – let's face it – out of the question. But we still have some good options.

Scan and copy. Copy the recipe cards and print them on card stock. If your scanner is high resolution, you can even preserve the smudges and splashes! (If you don't want to, there are companies who will do this for you.) Cut them out and arrange them in decorative tins. You can even insert copies of photos in with them, making a priceless gift people will treasure.

Have them printed. When you've scanned your recipe cards and clippings, consider uploading them to a printing company's website and having them arranged in a book. This preserves the look of the card itself, stains and handwriting included, and you can arrange the front and back of the cards side by side. The backgrounds of the pages can be family photos; you can have a lot of fun with this project! And the best part is that you can print as many as you like.

Laminate. If you're only keeping the cards for yourself, or after you've scanned them, the recipe cards can be laminated, but some say this may cause more damage over time.

Use a photo album! If you like the idea of protecting your original recipe cards but don't want to go to a lot of trouble, try an ordinary photo album! They're mostly acid-free these days, and you can easily arrange even the tiniest clippings on the pages. There will be lots of room for you to add a note about who the recipe came from and when, and even any special notes or observations you want to add.

Store them carefully. Keep the recipe cards out of the kitchen, in a dark, dry closet, in file folders. Keep newspaper clippings flat, not folded, and make sure they're separated from the recipe cards, as the ink can transfer.

***

Sometimes, family recipes aren't written down! If you're lucky enough to have grandparents (or elderly parents) still baking, it's time to think about how to record that information. So many family recipes have been taught in person and passed down that way, and may not actually be written anywhere. We have some tips for making sure those ways are not lost.

Make it! Ask to be shown. Watch how the dish is made, and pay attention. There is more to this than just the amounts of the ingredients, so listen to any comments about the texture of a dough or the thickness of a batter; these things are important.

Record it, if possible. There are so often stories or recollections associated with making certain dishes. If you can convince your subject to allow you to record the process on video, you'll capture so much more than just the recipe. We don't need to explain to you how valuable a video can be: hearing the explanation and stories while you work together in the kitchen, and also being able to see the person's face and watch their hands as they prepare the dish. Ask questions, and ask them to slow down if necessary.

And later, you can refer to the video for the details you may not have noticed, like the amounts of things and little tricks a person might not have thought to mention.

Whatever way we choose to record precious family heirloom recipes, one thing is sure: it's a great way to forge a connection between the women who raised us, and those we raise ourselves. Sometimes there won't be a way for them to know each other, but through sharing these recipes, our daughters (and sons) can hear the echoes of those who went before.

PIES

Chess Pie

Chess pie recipes appeared in American cookbooks during the mid-18th century and originates from England. It's a luscious custard filling of buttermilk, sugar, and eggs. This is my aunt Eunice recipe. It was passed down to her by her grandmother.

Serves 8 | Prep time 5 min. | Cook time 50-55 min.

Ingredients
1 baked 9-inch plain pie crust
Powdered sugar, for garnish

For the filling
2 cups sugar
2 tablespoons cornmeal
1 tablespoon flour
¼ teaspoon salt
½ cup butter or margarine, melted
¼ cup milk
1 tablespoon white vinegar
½ teaspoon vanilla extract
4 eggs, well beaten

Directions
1. Preheat the oven to 350°F.
2. In a bowl, combine the ingredients for the filling EXCEPT the eggs, whisking until well blended.
3. Stir in the eggs and stir to combine well.
4. Pour the mixture into the pie shell and place it in the oven.
5. After 10-15 minutes of baking, wrap the edges with aluminum foil and continue baking for 40-45 minutes.
6. Allow the pie to cool completely, then sift powdered sugar over the top if desired, and serve.

Jefferson Davis Pie

Created in the honor of President Jefferson during the civil war era, this pie is decadent and a close cousin to the chess pie consisting of a brown sugar custard with dates, raisins, and pecans. It's delicious and won't stay for long. I found this recipe in my aunt's recipe box and have done regularly over the years.

Serves 6-8 | Prep. time 10 min. | Cooking time 55 min.

Ingredients

½ cup golden raisins
½ cup chopped dates
½ cup pecans
3 tablespoons flour
1 teaspoon cinnamon
¼ teaspoon allspice
Pinch ground nutmeg
½ teaspoon salt
1 cup light brown sugar
1 stick unsalted butter, softened
1 cup light brown sugar
5 large egg yolks
1 ½ cups heavy cream
Blind baked 9-inch plain pastry shell
Whipped cream, for garnish

Directions

1. Preheat the oven to 325°F.
2. Place the raisins, dates, and pecans in a food processor or blender and run it until the mixture is finely ground. Spread this over the bottom of the pie shell.
3. Mix the flour, cinnamon, allspice, nutmeg, and salt together. Set it aside.
4. Cream the butter and brown sugar in a mixer. Add the yolks one at a time, mixing until well blended.
5. Add the flour mixture and cream alternately, stirring to combine.
6. Pour the filling into the pie shell.
7. Bake until the filling has thickened but is not too firm (about 55 minutes).
8. Serve chilled, topped with whipped cream.

Cherry-Peach Pandowdy

Pandowdy was a popular dessert in the 1800s, and we think it's time for it to make a comeback. It's like a cross between a cobbler and a pie.

Serves 12 | Prep. time 30 min. | Chilling time | Cooking time 30 min.

Ingredients
For the crust
2 cups all-purpose flour
1 tablespoon sugar
½ teaspoon salt
¾ cup cold unsalted butter, chopped
¼ cup cold vegetable shortening
4–5 tablespoons ice water

For the filling

2 ½ pounds peaches, pitted, peeled, and sliced, about 8 medium peaches (or about 6 cups frozen sliced peaches, thawed and drained from excess juices)

1 ½ pounds fresh or frozen (thawed) cherries, pitted

1 cup sugar

6 tablespoons all-purpose flour

1 teaspoon lemon zest

2 tablespoons fresh lemon juice

½ teaspoon salt

Egg wash

1 egg yolk

1 tablespoon water

Directions

1. Combine the flour, salt, and sugar in a mixing bowl, and mix briefly until combined. Cut in the butter and shortening until the mixture has pea-sized pieces. Gradually drizzle in the water just until the dough comes together.
2. Knead the dough a few times and shape it into a small rectangle, wrap, and refrigerate for 1 hour.
3. Preheat the oven to 400°F, and lightly coat an 11x8 baking or pie dish with butter.
4. Combine all the filling ingredients in a mixing bowl and pour them into the prepared pan.
5. Roll out the dough to a 12-inch square (it will be thick) and cut it in 16 pieces. Arrange the pieces over the filling, overlapping the edges.
6. Prepare the egg wash and brush it over the pastry.
7. Bake for 30 minutes, or until the filling is bubbly and the pastry is golden. Cover it with foil halfway through to prevent overbrowning, if needed.

Flapper Pie

Another wonderful recipe that has been lost in time. My grandmother on my father's side used to make it often for her family. It was on all the menus in dinners restaurant in the 1920s. This recipe was written on a piece of paper that I found in an old cookbook my grandma gave when I got married. I have made it a few times and it always impresses.

Serves 6-8 | Prep. time 20 min. | Cooking time 10-15 min

Ingredients
Graham Cracker Crust
1 ¼ cups graham cracker, finely crushed
¼ cup melted butter
½ cup sugar
Dash cinnamon

For the filling
2 ½ cups milk
½ cup white sugar
¼ cup cornstarch
3 egg yolks
1 teaspoon vanilla
Pinch salt
Meringue topping

Directions
To make the crust
1. Mix the ingredients thoroughly. Set aside 2 tablespoons for garnish.
2. Press the mixture into a pie pan to form a shell, and refrigerate to set.

To make the filling
3. In a saucepan, combine the filling ingredients and cook over medium heat, stirring constantly.
4. Continue cooking until the custard has thickened.
5. Allow the mixture to cool while preparing the meringue topping.

To assemble and bake
6. Preheat the oven to 350°F.
7. Spread the filling in the crust while it is still slightly warm, and spoon the meringue on top.
8. Swirl the meringue with a fork and swirl to form peaks.
9. Bake until the meringue is golden brown (about 10-15 minutes). Sprinkle with the reserved crust mixture to garnish.

Lemon Chess Pie with Sweet Berry Sauce

Here is a more sophisticated chess pie that were popular at the beginning of the 20th century with the addition of butter, coconut, lemons, berries. Tart and sweet, this southern classic is comfort food made from simple, wholesome ingredients.

Serves 8 | Prep. time 45 min. | Chill time 3 hours or more | Cooking time 35–40 min.

Ingredients
For the crust
1 cup all-purpose flour
½ cup sweetened shredded coconut
½ teaspoon salt

½ teaspoon cinnamon
⅓ cup cold butter, diced
3–4 tablespoons ice water

For the filling
6 large eggs, at room temperature
1 cup sugar
⅓ cup buttermilk
¼ cup lemon juice
3 tablespoons cornmeal
2 tablespoons grated lemon zest
¼ teaspoon salt
Pinch ground nutmeg
½ cup butter, melted

For the berry sauce
⅔ cup water
⅓ cup sugar
12 ounces frozen unsweetened mixed berries, thawed and drained
1 tablespoon lemon juice
Pinch salt

Directions
1. In a mixing bowl, combine the flour, coconut, salt, and cinnamon. Cut in the butter until a coarse meal is formed, while adding small splashes of water just until the crumbs are moist enough to form a dough.
2. Shape the dough into a disk and wrap it tightly in plastic. Refrigerate for at least 30 minutes.
3. Preheat the oven to 400°F.
4. Roll out the dough to ⅛-inch thickness for a 9-inch pan. Trim and flute the edges. Line the pastry with foil and cover it with dry beans or pie weights.

5. Bake for 8 minutes. Remove the foil and weights and cook another 8 minutes or so, until it is lightly golden. Set it aside to cool.
6. Turn the oven down to 325°F.
7. In a mixing bowl, whisk the eggs, sugar, buttermilk, lemon juice, cornmeal, lemon zest, salt, and nutmeg. Slowly mix in the melted butter.
8. Pour the filling into the crust and cover the edges with foil to prevent them from burning. Bake for 35 minutes, or until a knife inserted in the middle of the pie comes out clean.
9. Cool, and then refrigerate until chilled, at least 3 hours.
10. Prepare the sauce by combining the water and sugar in a small saucepan. Bring the mixture to a low boil and simmer until it is reduced to a quarter cup. Let it cool, and just before serving, stir in the berries.

Burnt Caramel Pie

If you'd like a change from the usual butterscotch pie, try this throwback family recipe of ours. It's delicious!

Makes 2 pies | Prep. time 30 min. | Chilling time 1 hour | Cooking time 30 min.

Ingredients
<u>For the crust</u>
2 ⅔ cups all-purpose flour
2 tablespoons sugar
½ teaspoon salt
½ cup cold, unsalted butter, cubed
6 tablespoons cold vegetable shortening

2 teaspoons vinegar
½ cup ice water

For the filling
4 eggs, separated
1 cup evaporated milk
½ cup light corn syrup
¼ cup butter, melted
½ teaspoon vanilla extract
3 cups white sugar, divided
½ cup all-purpose flour
3 cups water
½ teaspoon cream of tartar

Directions

1. Prepare the crusts. In a large bowl, combine the flour, sugar, and salt. Cut in the butter and vegetable shortening with a pastry cutter or two knives until the mixture has pea-sized crumbs.
2. Gradually mix in the water just until the dough comes together. Be careful not to overwork the dough. Divide it in half and shape both into disks. Wrap in plastic and refrigerate for at least an hour.
3. Preheat the oven to 375°F and set out two 9-inch pie plates.
4. Roll the dough into two 12-inch circles and arrange one in each pie plate. Trim and flute the edges. Place a piece of foil in each pastry shell and fill them with dry beans or pie weights.
5. Bake for 15 minutes and then remove the foil and weights. Continue to bake the crusts for 10 more minutes, or until golden. Set them aside to cool.
6. Combine the egg yolks, evaporated milk, syrup, melted butter, vanilla, half a cup of sugar, and flour.
7. Heat the oven to 325°F.

8. Heat a cast iron skillet and brown 2 cups of the sugar until golden. Remove the pan from the heat and stir in the water. Stir until the sugar dissolves, returning the skillet to the heat.

9. Whisk in the egg yolk mixture and cook until it thickens, and then five minutes more. Pour the filling into the prepared pie shells.

10. Beat the egg whites until foamy. Add the cream of tartar and gradually beat in the remaining half cup of sugar. Beat until stiff peaks form, and spread the meringue over the pies.

11. Bake for 15 minutes, until the meringue is golden.

My Mom's Vintage Rhubarb Pie

The *Old Boston Cookbook* was my mom's favorite. She used to make this amazing rhubarb pie from freshly trimmed rhubarb stalks from our homegrown plants. This recipe dates back to the 1920s and always brings back golden memories of going to cut the rhubarb in our garden and eating a piece of pie together with my mom as soon as it was ready. Sometimes, she would just do the regular crust and sometimes with a lattice pattern. I add coarse sugar on the top for added sweetness!

Serves 8 | Prep. time 10 min. | Cooking time 50 min.

Ingredients
2 tablespoons flour
2 eggs, beaten

3 cups rhubarb, chopped into ½-inch pieces
1 cup sugar
1 double crust pie crust of over 10-inch in diameter
Egg wash (whisk 1 egg and 2 tablespoons of water)

Directions

1. Preheat the oven to 425°F. Grease a 9-inch pie pan with melted butter or cooking spray.
2. Mix all the filling ingredients in a medium bowl. Combine well.
3. Arrange the bottom pie crust over the pie pan and spoon the filling mixture into it.
4. Place the top crust atop the filling and crimp the edges together with the bottom crust. Cut off the extra dough if needed
5. Cut some holes in the top crust for steam to escape. Brush some of the egg wash lightly on the crust top.
6. Bake for 15 minutes.
7. Turn down the temperature to 325°F and bake for 30-45 minutes more, until the top is evenly golden.
8. Serve warm.

Note: For a lattice pattern, lay the top crust flat on a flour dusted cutting and cut even strips of dough of ½ to ¾ -inch wide. I use a ruler and a pizza cutter for this step. Place half of the dough strips over the pie's rhubarb filling, in parallel lines, spaced evenly. From the middle, fold over every other strip to the same side. Lay a strip of dough perpendicular to the already placed strips to start your weaving pattern in the middle of the pie, at the fold. Fold the strips back down over the just placed strip. Fold the other strips that were not the first time over the strip that was just placed and lay another strip of dough at the fold. And continue in this fashion until all the pie is covered. Crimp the edges of the strip with the bottom crust.

Apricot Icebox Pie

This recipe comes from an old, yellowed card in my Aunt Kristie's recipe box—I think it's from the 1970s. It's different and fresh, and you're going to love it.

Serves 8 | Prep. time 30 min. plus chilling time | Cooking time 15 min.

Ingredients
For the crust

48 vanilla wafers, crushed

½ cup margarine, melted

For the filling

1 ½ cups icing sugar

¾ cup margarine, melted

3 eggs, beaten

1 ½ cups heavy cream
¼ cup sugar
½ cup chopped pecans
2 (13-ounce) cans apricot halves

Directions

1. Crush the wafers and mix in the melted margarine. Press the base into a 9-inch pie plate and chill until set.
2. In a medium saucepan, combine the icing sugar, margarine, and eggs. Cook over medium heat, stirring constantly, until thickened. Set the pot aside and let it cool a little.
3. Drain the apricots and cut into bitesize pieces.
4. In a separate bowl, whip the cream until it begins to thicken, and gradually incorporate the ¼ cup of sugar. Beat until stiff peaks form. Fold in the apricots and pecans with a spatula.
5. To assemble the pie, place the cooked filling on the bottom, top with the apricot whipped cream.
6. Chill one hour before serving.

Angel Pie

Angel pie dates back to the 1930s and the recipe has been passed down to the next generation. The pudding flavor can differ from cook to cook. My grandmother used to make it with lemons. And this is her recipe. If you like meringue, this will definitively be a hit in your family. You need to plan ahead for this pie as the filling should be refrigerated at least 8 hours before serving.

Serves 8 | Chill time 8 hours | Prep. time 15 min.|
Cooking time 8 min.

Ingredients
For the meringue pie crust

Butter and flour for greasing and dusting

3 extra large egg whites

1 pinch cream of tartar

1 teaspoon pure vanilla extract

¾ cup white sugar

For the lemon filling

5 egg yolks

½ cup sugar

¼ cup lemon juice

Zest of 1 lemon

1 cup

Whipped Cream Topping

1 cup heavy cream, chilled

2-4 tablespoons confectioner's sugar

1 teaspoon vanilla

Gelatin to stabilize cream (optional)

¼ tablespoon water

Directions
For the meringue pie crust

1. Pre-heat the oven to 275⁰F and place oven rack in the middle position.
2. Coat a 10-inch deep pie pan with butter and lightly flour the pan. A glass pie pan such as Pyrex works best. Remove excess flour by reversing the pan over the sink.
3. In an electric stand mixer with the whisk attachment on, add the egg whites, vanilla, and a pinch of tartar. Beat on low speed until foamy.
4. Increase speed to high and gradually add the sugar. Beat until stiff peaks form.

5. Spread the meringue evenly into the pie dish with a spatula or the back of a wooden spoon.
6. Place into the oven and bake for 1 hour. Turn off the oven and let the meringue shell rest in the oven for 1 more hour. Make sure not to open the oven door as the meringue continues to dry up.
7. Remove from the oven and let cool completely.

For the lemon filling
8. While the pie shell is cooling down, prepare the filling.
9. Beat the yolks until they are thickened, and heat them gently in a double boiler.
10. While continuously beating, add the sugar, lemon juice, and zest.
11. Continue cooking and stirring until the filling is lightly colored and thick.
12. Remove the mixture from the heat and let it cool completely.
13. Add the lemon filling to the meringue pie crust, cover with plastic wrap, and refrigerate for at least 8 hours and up to 12 hours.

For the topping
14. If you are using gelatin, heat the water and add the gelatin, stirring until it is completely dissolved.
15. Let the gelatin cool down a little, but don't let it set.
16. Whip the cream to soft peaks, and gradually add the sugar and vanilla while whipping.
17. Add the gelatin in a thin stream while whipping continuously.

To assemble
18. Take 1 cup of the whipped cream topping and gently fold it into the lemon filling.
19. Fill the meringue crust with the rest of the filling.
20. Spoon the remaining whipped cream topping over the filling, and chill.

Sawdust Pie

Serves 8 | Prep time 5 min. | Cook time 35 min.

Ingredients
Blind baked 9-inch plain pastry pie shell

For the filling
1 ½ cups desiccated coconut
1 ½ cups graham cracker crumbs
1 ½ cups pecans, chopped
1 ½ cups sugar
1 cup egg whites

Directions
1. Preheat the oven to 350°F.
2. In a bowl, mix the ingredients for the filling EXCEPT the egg whites.
3. Beat the egg whites just until they are foamy, and stir them into the coconut mixture.
4. Pour it into the pie shell.
5. Bake until set (about 35 minutes).

Italian Easter Pie

Easter Pie comes in many varieties, some savory and some sweet. This is an old family recipe that has probably been changed subtly over time, and now includes chocolate chips as well as more traditional ingredients like citron.

Serves 6–8 | Prep. time 25 min. plus chilling time | Cooking time 55 min.

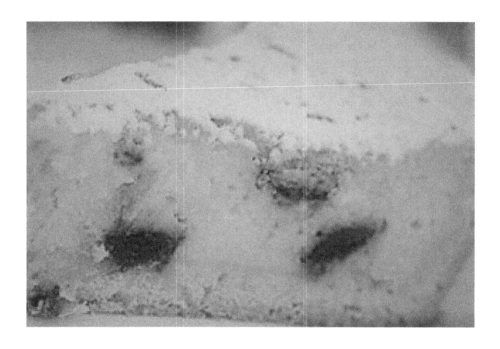

Ingredients

<u>For the crust</u>

1 ⅔ cups all-purpose flour

2 tablespoons sugar

¼ teaspoon salt

¼ teaspoon baking powder

½ cup butter

2 large eggs, lightly beaten
Icing sugar for dusting

For the filling
2 cups ricotta cheese
1 cup sugar
1 tablespoon cornstarch
½ teaspoon grated lemon zest
½ teaspoon grated orange zest
¼ teaspoon salt
4 large eggs
2 teaspoons vanilla extract
⅓ cup semisweet chocolate chips
⅓ cup diced citron, optional
Pinch ground cinnamon
Pinch ground nutmeg

Directions
1. In a mixing bowl, combine the flour, sugar, salt, and baking powder. Mix well.
2. Cut in the butter until a coarse meal is formed. Add the eggs and mix until the pastry comes together. Wrap and refrigerate for one hour.
3. Roll out the dough for a 9-inch pie plate. Trim and flute the edges. Refrigerate until ready to use.
4. Preheat the oven to 350°F.
5. To make the filling, beat the ricotta with the sugar and cornstarch. Mix in the lemon and orange zest and the salt.
6. In a separate bowl, beat the eggs until they are thick and pale yellow, about 5 minutes. Gently fold them into the ricotta mixture together with the remaining ingredients.
7. Pour the filling into the crust and bake for 55 minutes, or until a knife inserted in the center comes out clean.
8. Let cool and refrigerate for 1 hour prior to serving. Dust pie with icing sugar before serving.

Old-Fashioned Buttermilk Pie

Buttermilk pie is a silky custard-like pie using buttermilk and eggs, that came from English settlers at the end of the 18th century. My grandmother used to make it to finish up a buttermilk carton when I was a child. This is her recipe.

Serves 6-8 | Prep time 20 min. | Cook time 1 hour 45 min.

Ingredients
3 tablespoons unsalted butter
1 ¼ cups white sugar
3 eggs
1 tablespoon flour
½ cup buttermilk
1 teaspoon vanilla
Unbaked 9-inch pie shell, plain pastry

Directions

1. Preheat the oven to 300°F.
2. In a mixing bowl, cream together the butter and sugar.
3. Stir in the eggs, flour, buttermilk, and vanilla. Blend well.
4. Spread the filling in the pie shell.
5. Bake for about 1 hour and 45 minutes, or until a knife inserted in the filling comes out clean.
6. Let the pie cool before serving.

Hillbilly Pie

Similar to the Oatmeal pie, this old recipe from the Ozarks is so easy to prepare with fewer ingredients and the kids love to help me make it!

Serves 8 | Prep. time 10 min | Cooking time 1 hour

Ingredients

¾ cup light corn syrup
¾ cup white sugar
3 eggs
1 cup rolled oats
¼ cup margarine or butter, melted
2 teaspoons vanilla extract
1 (9-inch) unbaked pie crust

Directions

1. Preheat the oven to 350°F.
2. In a mixing bowl, combine the corn syrup, white sugar, eggs, oats, margarine (or butter), and vanilla.
3. Pour this mixture into the pie crust, and bake for 1 hour, or until a knife inserted in the center comes out clean.

Banana Cream Pie

When the summer comes and the antique cars take to the roads again, I sometimes think about the lifestyle those people are remembering – the 1950s, and the days of sock hops and diners. This recipe hails from then, and it's just the sort of thing you might order in one of those classic diners.

Serves 6 | Prep. time 10 min. | Chill time 6 hours | Cooking time 30 min.

Ingredients
For the crust
1 ¼ cups all-purpose flour
¾ teaspoon salt
1 tablespoon sugar
½ cup butter, cold
2–4 tablespoons ice water

For the filling
1 cup sugar
⅓ cup cornstarch
1 teaspoon salt
3 cups whole milk
4 egg yolks, beaten
3 tablespoons butter
1 teaspoon vanilla extract
2–3 bananas, sliced
Topping
2–3 cups whipped cream, for topping

Directions

1. Make the crust. Preheat the oven to 375°F.
2. In a mixing bowl, combine the flour, salt, and sugar. Cut in the butter until none of the lumps are larger than a pea.
3. Add the ice water little by little, mixing with a fork, until the pastry is moist enough to cling together and form a ball.
4. Roll out the dough, and arrange it in a 9-inch pie plate. Trim and flute the edges, and pierce bottom with a fork.
5. Bake 10–12 minutes, or until the crust is golden brown. Set it aside to cool
6. In a saucepan, prepare the filling. Mix the sugar, cornstarch, salt, and milk. Cook until it bubbles, stirring constantly.
7. Beat the egg yolks, and then stir in a small amount of the hot filling, whisking constantly, to temper the egg. Add a bit more and mix until smooth, and then add this back to the pot.
8. Bring the pot to a slow boil, and stir for two minutes.
9. Add the butter and vanilla, and refrigerate for 30 minutes.
10. Spoon half the pudding into the cooled crust, and cover with banana slices. Add the rest of the pudding, cover, and refrigerate until set, at least 6 hours.
11. Serve topped with whipped cream.

Tyler Pie

This pie was served at the White House during President John Tyler tenure at the end of the 19th century. It was an old family recipe passed down from one generation to the next and originated in England. It's a rich custard pie that melts in your mouth. A favorite in our family too!

Serves 8 | Prep time 10 min. | Cook time 35-40 min.

Ingredients
1 cup sugar
½ teaspoon of flour
Pinch salt
2 eggs
1 teaspoon vanilla extract
½ teaspoon lemon extract
Pinch nutmeg
½ cup butter, slightly melted
1 cups milk
9-inch plain pastry pie shell

Directions
1. Preheat the oven to 350°F.
2. Combine the sugar, flour, and salt, and mix well.
3. In a separate bowl, beat the eggs and add the vanilla, lemon extract (optional), nutmeg, and butter. Stir in the sugar mixture.
4. Finally, mix in the milk.
5. Pour the filling into an unbaked pie shell.
6. Bake until set and nicely browned (about 35-40 minutes).

Vinegar Pie

Cooks from the 19th century started using vinegar to flavor pies, especially in the North and Midwest of the Unites States. Vinegar was used to add a tart flavor to desserts when citrus, especially lemons were not available. I found this recipe in my grandmother's recipe box and it seriously tastes like a lemon pie!

Serves 8 | Prep time 15 min. | Cook time 35 min.

Ingredients
3 tablespoons flour
1 cup sugar
⅓ cup white vinegar
1 ⅔ cups hot water
1 egg, well beaten
1 teaspoon lemon extract

2 tablespoons butter
Pre-baked 9-inch plain pastry shell, cooled
Meringue Topping

Directions

1. Preheat the oven to 325°F.
2. Combine the sugar with the flour in a double boiler.
3. Whisk in the vinegar, water, egg, and lemon flavor.
4. Cook, stirring, in the double boiler until the mixture is thick.
5. Remove from the heat and stir in the butter.
6. Pour the filling into the pie shell.
7. If desired, pile the meringue topping on the filling and spread to the edges of the pie. Use a fork or a piping bag to create swirls and peaks.
8. Bake until the meringue is golden brown, about 15 minutes.
9. Serve hot.

Mincemeat Tarts

Traditionally made at Christmas, these are treats that are well worth the effort. Canned or bottled mincemeat has simplified many recipes, but today we'll show you how to make the filling from scratch.

Serves 36 | Prep. time 30 min. | Chill time 1 hour | Cooking time 1 hour.

Ingredients

For the filling

3 large apples, coarsely grated

1 pear, finely chopped

Zest and juice of 1 lemon

Zest and juice of 1 orange
1 cup raisins
1 cup golden raisins
1 cup currants
½ cup candied peel
1 ¼ cups dark brown sugar
⅓ cup butter
1 teaspoon ground cinnamon
¼ teaspoon allspice
¼ teaspoon nutmeg
¼ teaspoon salt

For the pastry
2 ½ cups all-purpose flour
¼ teaspoon salt
1 tablespoon sugar
1 cup butter, frozen
1 cup ice water

Directions
1. Combine all the ingredients for the filling in a large saucepan and bring the mixture to a simmer. Cook on medium-low for 20–30 minutes, stirring often, until the mixture is thick and fragrant.
2. Set the filling aside to cool.
3. In a large bowl, combine the flour, salt, and sugar. Using a cheese grater, grate the butter into the flour and mix well.
4. Gradually add the water until a dough forms, being careful not to overwork the pastry.
5. Wrap and refrigerate the dough for one hour.
6. Preheat the oven to 400°F and set out 3 ungreased muffin pans.

7. On a lightly floured surface, roll out the dough and cut it into 2-inch circles. Fit them into muffin tins, and fill each with 2 tablespoons of mincemeat filling.
8. If there is leftover dough, use a 1-inch cutter of your choice to make shapes for the tops of the tarts.
9. Bake for about 15 minutes, until the pastry is golden brown.
10. Cool, and serve.

Indiana Sugar Cream Pie

One of the things I love about vintage recipes is that they use ingredients we tend to have on hand. This recipe, for instance, is a good choice when you feel like having custard, but don't have (or want to use) any eggs. We suggest good quality cream, vanilla, and nutmeg—but in the spirit of the recipe, use what you have.

Serves 8 | Prep. time 10 min. | Cooking time 40 min.

Ingredients

For the crust

1 ⅔ cups all-purpose flour

2 tablespoons sugar

¼ teaspoon salt

¼ teaspoon baking powder

½ cup butter

2 large eggs, lightly beaten

For the filling

1 ½ cups heavy cream

½ cup milk

1 teaspoon vanilla extract

½ cup all-purpose flour

1 cup sugar

½ teaspoon salt

1 tablespoon butter, finely chopped

Freshly grated nutmeg

Directions

1. In a mixing bowl, combine the flour, sugar, salt, and baking powder. Mix well.
2. Cut in the butter until a coarse meal is formed. Add the eggs and mix until the pastry comes together. Wrap and refrigerate for one hour.
3. Roll out the dough for a 9-inch pie plate. Trim and flute the edges. Place the pie shell in the freezer.
4. Preheat the oven to 425°F.
5. Make the filling. In a bowl, mix the cream, milk, and vanilla.
6. In a separate bowl, combine the flour, sugar, and salt.
7. Slowly whisk the milk mixture into the flour mixture until combined.

8. Remove the pie crust from the freezer. Scatter the butter pieces over the bottom of the crust, and season with some nutmeg.

9. Whisk the batter again and carefully pour it into the crust. Place the pie on the middle rack in the preheated oven.

10. Bake for 10 minutes, and then open the oven door. Using a fork, carefully stir the filling, being careful not to damage the bottom of the pie.

11. Turn the heat down to 325°F and bake until it is set, about 30 minutes.

12. Remove the pie to a cooling rack and sprinkle with some more nutmeg. Cool, and serve.

Strawberry Chiffon Pie

The difference between a chiffon pie and a cream pie is that the chiffon uses gelatin and meringue in the filling rather than only cream. Traditional recipes – these pies go back to the 1920s – might have you beat fresh egg whites, but this one uses meringue powder - a safer bet if you're concerned about salmonella bacteria.

Serves 6-8 | Chill time 4 hours | Prep. time 25 min. | Cooking time 10 min.

Ingredients
For the crust
18 graham crackers, crushed
⅓ cup butter, melted
¼ cup sugar

For the pie filling
1 pint fresh strawberries
½ cup sugar
1 tablespoon unflavored gelatin
¼ cup cold water
½ cup very hot water
1 tablespoon lemon juice
Pinch salt
1 cup whipped cream
1 ½ tablespoons meringue powder
¼ cup water
¼ cup sugar, divided

Directions

1. Preheat the oven to 375°F.
2. Crush the graham crackers and stir in the melted butter and sugar. Press the mixture into 9-inch pie plate to form the crust.
3. Bake for 10 minutes, and then set it aside to cool.
4. Meanwhile, crush the strawberries and stir in the sugar. Set aside for 30 minutes.
5. In a clean bowl, pour the cold water over the gelatin to soften it, and then add the hot water to dissolve it.
6. Add the lemon juice and salt to the strawberries. Stir in the dissolved gelatin.
7. Chill for about an hour, until the berry mixture begins to hold its shape a little when you move it with a spoon.
8. Fold the whipped cream into the berry mixture.
9. Beat the meringue powder with the water and half the sugar until soft peaks form. Slowly add the rest of the sugar and continue beating just until stiff peaks form.
10. Fold the meringue mixture into the strawberry mixture, and spread it in the prepared crust. Refrigerate until firm.
11. Top with additional whipped cream, if desired.

Lemonade Icebox Pie

This American southern classic tastes like summer. The fresh, tart sweetness of the creamy pie with the crisp graham crust is a real treat for the taste buds!

Serves 8 | Prep. time 10 min. | Cooking time 0 min.

Ingredients

8 ounces cream cheese, softened

1 (14-ounce) can sweetened condensed milk

¾ cup lemonade concentrate, thawed

½ teaspoon vanilla extract

Pinch salt

8 ounces frozen whipped topping, thawed

2 drops yellow food coloring, optional

1 (9-inch) prepared graham cracker crust

Lemon slices (well drained) or zest for serving

Directions

1. In a mixing bowl, beat the cream cheese and sweetened condensed milk together until thoroughly combined.
2. Add the lemonade concentrate, vanilla, and salt. Mix well.
3. Fold in the whipped topping and food coloring, if using.
4. Spoon the pie filling into the crust and freeze until set.
5. Garnish with lemon slices or zest, and serve.

Marlborough Pie

The creation of the Marborough pie is traced back to British chef Robert May's 1660 cookbook The Accomplished Cook. It was introduced to America during the 17th century as a special treat to celebrate the harvest and has been shared during Thanksgiving meals ever since.

Serves 8 | Prep time 10 min. plus 4 hours cooling time | Cook time 1 hour

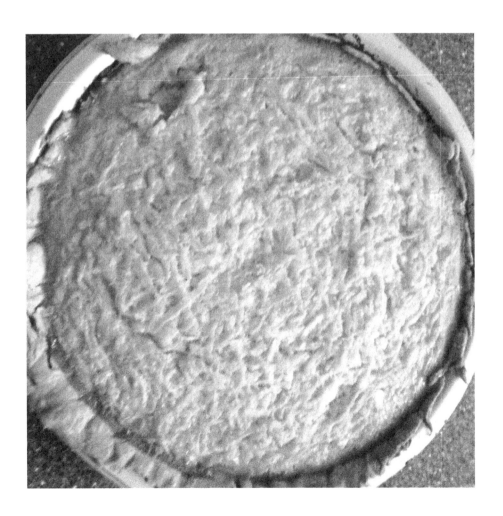

Ingredients

1 baked 9-inch pie crust

4 tablespoons butter

4 cups apple, peeled and shredded (combine Granny Smith Apples with sweeter varieties)

½ cup sugar

¼ teaspoon cinnamon

¼ teaspoon nutmeg

¼ teaspoon salt

3 eggs, lightly beaten

½ cup heavy cream

5 tablespoons dry sherry

1 teaspoon grated lemon zest

1 teaspoon vanilla extract

Whipped cream, as garnish

Directions

1. Preheat the oven to 325°F.
2. Melt the butter in a skillet over medium heat.
3. Add the shredded apples and cook, stirring frequently, for 15 minutes. The mixture should be very dry, with almost all the liquid evaporated.
4. Let it cool.
5. Combine the sugar, cinnamon, nutmeg and salt in a large bowl.
6. Whisk in the eggs, cream, sherry, lemon zest, and vanilla, and mix until smooth.
7. Stir in the apples, and transfer the mixture to a pie shell.
8. Bake until set (about 40 minutes).
9. Remove the pie from the oven and set it on a rack. Let cool for about 4 hours.
10. Chill, and serve with whipped cream.

Bakewell Tart

What the heck is a Bakewell Tart? It's a traditional English dessert, basically a jam and almond pie. With frangipane. What's frangipane? Almond custard. Let's get started.

Serves 8 | Prep. time 45 min. | Chilling time 7 hours | Cooking time 1 hour

Ingredients
For the dough
½ cup butter, room temperature
⅔ cup icing sugar, sifted
2 cups flour, sifted
2 large eggs

¼ cup raspberry jam

For the filling
¾ cup butter, room temperature
¾ cup sugar
3 eggs
3 tablespoons flour
1 ¾ cups almond flour
1 teaspoon almond extract
¼ cup sliced almonds

Directions

1. Combine the butter and icing sugar and beat until smooth. Mix in one egg and about ¾ cup of flour. Continue mixing and adding flour gradually until a dough forms. Do not overmix. Wrap and refrigerate the dough for 6 hours.
2. Thirty minutes before continuing, remove the dough from the fridge.
3. Dust a clean work surface with flour and roll the dough to a ¼-inch thickness for a 10-inch tart pan. Trim the edges and reserve the extra dough.
4. Prick the bottom of the pie and refrigerate for 1 hour.
5. Preheat the oven to 375°F. Cover the dough with parchment and fill it with dry beans. Bake for 15 minutes.
6. Remove the crust from the oven and take out the beans and parchment. Use the leftover dough to fill any cracks.
7. Beat the remaining egg and brush it over the whole inside of the crust. Return the crust to the oven and bake for 5 minutes, until lightly golden.
8. When the shell has cooled completely, spread the jam in.
9. Preheat the oven to 350°F.
10. Make the frangipane filling. Beat the butter with the sugar until the mixture becomes white and firm. Mix in the eggs one at a time, then the flour, almond flour, and extract.
11. Spread the filling over the jam, being careful not to disturb the jam. Sprinkle the sliced almonds on top.
12. Bake for 45 minutes. Cool completely before slicing.

CAKES AND CUPCAKES

Baked Alaska

The baked Alaska was invented a long time ago in 1867 and is such an elegant dessert. It still popular today for any celebration. It was created to celebrate USA's purchase of Alaska by renown chef Charles Ranhofer, from the Delmonico's restaurant in New York city. He first named it the Alaska-Florida cake. Later the name was changed to the Baked Alaska as we know it today. How can something that looks so spectacular be so easy to make?

Serves 8 | Prep. time 20 min. | Freezing time 3 hours | Cooking time 2-5 minutes

Ingredients

8 cups Neapolitan ice cream, softened 20 minutes (or your choice of flavors)
1 prepared pound cake, cut in 1" slices
6 egg whites, at room temperature
¼ teaspoon cream of tartar
½ cup sugar

Directions

1. Set out a 3-quart bowl, and line it with plastic wrap.
2. Spoon the ice cream into the bowl, pressing it to eliminate any air pockets, and arranging the flavors so each serving will get more than one kind of ice cream.
3. Top the ice cream with slices of pound cake, covering the whole surface of the bowl.
4. Cover, and freeze for at least 3 hours.
5. Preheat the oven broiler and place oven rack in lowest position.
6. Beat the egg whites with the cream of tartar until soft peaks form. Gradually add the sugar and beat until stiff peaks form.
7. Remove the bowl from the freezer and take off the wrap. Invert the dish onto a baking pan, and cover with meringue. Use a knife or the back of a spoon to make a pattern.
8. Broil for 2–5 minutes, until the meringue is golden. Let it rest a few minutes before serving.

Note: If you have a culinary torch, you can use it to brown the meringue instead of broiling in the oven.

Hot Milk Cake

This Depression-era cake is as wholesome and comforting as it sounds. It's good alone or with a fruit compote, and it's a delicious choice for trifle.

Serves 12–16 | Prep. time 20 min. | Cooking time 30 min.

Ingredients
4 large eggs
2 cups sugar
1 ½ teaspoon vanilla extract
2 ¼ cups all-purpose flour
2 ¼ teaspoons baking powder
1 ¼ cups 2% milk
⅔ cup salted butter, cubed
Icing sugar, for dusting

Directions

1. Preheat the oven to 350°F and butter a 9x13 pan.
2. In a mixing bowl, beat the eggs for about 5 minutes, until they are thick and lemony yellow. Gradually add the sugar and vanilla, and beat until light and fluffy.
3. Combine the flour and baking powder, and gradually incorporate them into the batter.
4. In a saucepan, heat the milk and add the butter. When the butter has melted and the milk is steamy, add it to the batter and mix until just combined.
5. Pour the batter into the prepared pan and bake for 30 minutes. The cake is done when a toothpick inserted in the center comes out clean.
6. Cool, and dust with icing sugar.

Jam Roly Poly with Custard

This old English dessert was sometimes called "shirt-sleeve pudding" because it was steamed in the sleeve of a shirt. We think we'll just bake ours in the oven.

Serves 6 | Prep. time 20 min. | Cooking time 35–40 min.

Ingredients

1 ¾ cups all-purpose flour
2 ½ teaspoons baking powder
¾ teaspoon salt
1 cup shredded suet (4 ounces)
½ cup water
¼ cup jam of your choice
1 egg, beaten
1 tablespoon milk
Caster sugar for sprinkling
For the custard
6 egg yolks
⅓ cup sugar
1 ¼ cups whole milk
1 teaspoon vanilla extract

Directions

1. Preheat the oven to 400°F and butter a 9x13 baking pan.
2. In a mixing bowl, combine the flour, baking powder, and salt. Stir in the suet.
3. Gradually add the water and stir to moisten.
4. Turn out the dough onto a lightly floured surface and roll it into a 12x10 inch rectangle.
5. Spread the jam onto the dough. (Tip: heating it a little might help if it's too thick to spread.)
6. Starting on the long side near you, carefully roll up the dough and pinch the seam. Transfer the roll to the buttered dish.
7. Combine the egg with the milk, and brush the cake roll with it. Sprinkle generously with caster sugar.
8. Bake on the center rack for 35–40 minutes, until golden.
9. Meanwhile, prepare the custard. In a heatproof bowl, beat the egg yolks with the sugar until creamy.
10. Heat the milk in a saucepan until steamy and add the vanilla.
11. Place the egg bowl over a pot of simmering water. Slowly add the milk mixture, whisking constantly. Cook, stirring, until it thickens.
12. Serve the cake roll with warm custard.

Pineapple Upside-Down Cake

Hawaiian pineapple became a hit in America in the 1920s because it was easy to ship in cans, and ladies' magazines of the day loved to feature recipes for ways to use it. Couple this delicious fruit with a traditional sponge cake and a cast iron skillet, and you've got the classic we still love today.

Serves 8 | Prep. time 15 min. | Cooking time 45 min.

Ingredients
2 cups all-purpose flour
2 teaspoons baking powder
½ teaspoon salt
2 large eggs, separated
½ cup butter, softened
1 cup granulated sugar

61

½ cup whole milk
1 ½ teaspoons vanilla extract

For the topping
3 tablespoons butter
1 cup paced brown sugar
6–8 pineapple rings, canned
6–8 maraschino cherries (more if desired)

Directions

1. Preheat the oven to 350°F.
2. Prepare the topping in a 10-inch cast iron skillet by melting the butter and sugar together over medium heat. When the sugar is dissolved, arrange the pineapple rings in the caramel and place a cherry inside each*. (Add more if you like.) Set the skillet aside.
3. Sift together the flour, baking powder, and salt, and set them aside.
4. In a clean bowl, beat the egg whites until they are light and frothy.
5. In a separate bowl, beat the sugar with the butter until it is fluffy. Add the egg yolks, and mix them in.
6. Add the milk in increments, alternating with the dry ingredients.
7. Fold in the vanilla and egg whites.
8. Spoon the batter over the pineapple and bake for 45 minutes, or until a toothpick inserted in the center comes out clean.
9. Loosen the edges with a knife, and carefully flip the cake onto a serving plate.
10. If you haven't added the cherries, do so now.
11. Cool, and serve!

*Some people prefer to add the cherries after the cake is baked.

Lemony Cupcakes

My grandmother used to make these, and even though I wasn't a big fan of lemon, I loved them. She said her mother used this recipe as far back as the 1920s.

Serves 24 | Prep. time 15 min. | Cooking time 17–20 min.

Ingredients
2 cups sugar
¾ cup butter
3 eggs
1 cup milk
¼ cup lemon juice
3 cups all-purpose flour
1 teaspoon cream of tartar
½ teaspoon salt
½ teaspoon baking soda

<u>Lemon Cream Cheese Frosting</u>
1 (8 ounce) package cream cheese, softened
¼ cup butter
2 tablespoons lemon juice
2 teaspoons lemon zest
1 teaspoon vanilla extract
5 cups icing sugar

Directions

1. Preheat the oven to 375°F and prepare a muffin tin with butter or paper cups.
2. In a mixing bowl, combine the butter and sugar until creamy. Add the eggs one at a time, beating well after each addition.
3. Add the milk and lemon juice and mix well.
4. Sift the dry ingredients together and add them to the batter. Mix just until combined.
5. Spoon the batter into the prepared cups, and bake for 17–20 minutes until done.
6. Meanwhile, prepare the frosting. Beat all the ingredients together until smooth.
7. Frost the cupcakes when they are completely cool.

Amish Applesauce Cake

This moist and fragrant cake has been bringing the kids to the kitchen for over a hundred years.

Serves 12 | Prep. time 15 min. | Cooking time 30 min.

Ingredients
1 cup sugar
½ cup butter, softened
2 eggs

2 cups all-purpose flour
1 teaspoon ground cinnamon
¼ teaspoon nutmeg
¼ teaspoon cardamom
1 teaspoon baking soda
½ teaspoon salt
1 ½ cups applesauce
1 teaspoon vanilla extract

Directions

1. Preheat the oven to 350°F and butter a 9x13 baking dish.
2. In a mixing bowl, beat the sugar and butter until fluffy. Mix in the eggs one at a time.
3. Stir in the flour, cinnamon, nutmeg, cardamom, baking soda, and salt. Add the applesauce and vanilla, and mix well.
4. Bake for 30–35 minutes, or until a toothpick inserted in the center of the cake comes out clean.

Chocolate and Cream Icebox Cake

This beautiful icebox cake dessert looks simply irresistible and has such a soft, creamy texture that it melts in your mouth.

Serves 12 | Prep. time 15 min. | Chill time 4–6 hours

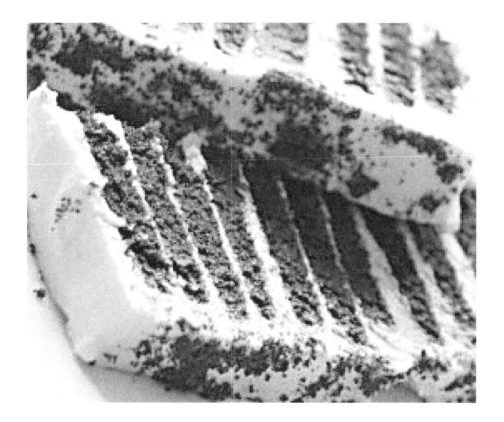

Ingredients
2 tablespoons confectioners' sugar
2 cups heavy whipping cream
1 teaspoon vanilla extract
1 (9-ounce) package chocolate wafers
Chocolate curls (optional)

Directions

1. Beat the cream in a large mixing bowl until soft peaks form.
2. Add the vanilla and sugar. Combine well.
3. Spread the cream mixture over the chocolate wafers.
4. Stack the wafers one by one to make six stacks.
5. Turn these stacks on their edges and place them on a serving platter to make a long rectangular cake.
6. Spread the remaining cream on the sides and top. Add chocolate curls on top if desired.
7. Refrigerate for 4–6 hours and serve chilled.

Lazy Daisy Cake

In the early 1900s, food in America was changing. Baking became easier with the advent of the gas stove, and with the population becoming more diverse, new ingredients were appearing. In 1914, a recipe for Lazy Daisy cake appeared in the Chicago Sunday Tribune.

Serves 12 | Prep. time 20 min. | Cooking time 35 min.

Ingredients
For the cake
2 cups all-purpose flour
2 teaspoons baking powder
½ teaspoon salt
1 cup milk
¼ cup butter

1 teaspoon vanilla extract
4 eggs, room temperature
2 cups sugar

For the topping
½ cup butter, melted
¾ cup packed brown sugar
6 tablespoons evaporated milk
1 ½ cups shredded coconut
½ teaspoon salt

Directions

1. Preheat the oven to 350°F and butter two 9-inch cake pans.
2. In a mixing bowl, combine the flour, baking powder, and salt.
3. In a saucepan, heat the milk and add the butter. Cook until the butter melts. Add the vanilla.
4. In a separate bowl, beat the eggs with the sugar until pale and thick. Gradually fold in the dry and wet ingredients alternatively, until just combined.
5. Pour the batter into the prepared cake pans and bake until set, 30–35 minutes.
6. Allow the cakes to cool slightly while you preheat the broiler.
7. To make the topping, combine the ingredients in a mixing bowl. Spoon the topping onto the cakes and gently spread it out. Brown them under the broiler for 3–4 minutes, being careful not to let them burn.
8. Serve warm.

Tunnel of Fudge Cake

This is an early version of the lava cakes we love, except it's not runny. If you love chocolate and walnuts, this is the recipe to try. We're told it originally came from a flour package.

Serves 12 | Prep. time 15 min. | Cooking time 45–50 min.

Ingredients
1 ¾ cups margarine, softened
1 ¾ cups white sugar
6 eggs
1 teaspoon vanilla extract
2 cups icing sugar
2 ¼ cups all-purpose flour
¾ cup unsweetened cocoa powder
2 cups chopped walnuts

For the glaze
¾ cup icing sugar
¼ cup unsweetened cocoa powder
2 tablespoons milk

Directions

1. Preheat the oven to 350°F. Butter or grease a 10-inch Bundt pan.
2. In a mixing bowl, beat the butter and sugar until fluffy. Crack in the eggs one at a time, mixing well after each. Add the vanilla.
3. Gradually incorporate the 2 cups of icing sugar, and then the flour and cocoa.
4. Stir in the walnuts and spread the batter in the pan.
5. Bake for 45–50 minutes, until the top has set and the edges are pulling away from the pan. Cool in the pan for 1 ½ hours, and then on a rack for another 2–3 hours.
6. To make the glaze, mix the icing sugar and cocoa together. Add just enough milk to make the consistency you need to drizzle. Spoon it over the cake.

Holiday Cake

This is a traditional recipe for a lovely, simple cake, courtesy of the English. It's very good with a hot cup of tea. In the early 1900s and before, it was common to sweeten baked goods with raisins and currants.

Serves 12 | Prep. time 15 min. | Cooking time 2 hours

Ingredients

3 ½ cups all-purpose flour, sifted
2 teaspoons baking powder
1 teaspoon salt
1 cup chopped almonds
1 cup raisins
¼ cup lemon peel, cut fine
1 cup butter or other shortening
2 cups sugar
1 ½ cups shredded coconut
2 teaspoons vanilla
1 teaspoon almond extract
10 egg whites, stiffly beaten

Directions

1. Preheat the oven to 250°F and grease an angel food pan. Line the bottom with paper.
2. Sift the flour with the baking powder and salt, then sift again three times to combine. Sprinkle ½ cup over the fruits and mix well.
3. Cream the butter with the sugar and mix well. Add the remaining flour a little at a time.
4. Add the coconut, floured fruits, vanilla, and almond extract. Fold in the egg whites.
5. Transfer the batter to the pan and bake for 2 hours.

Sunshine Cake

How about shining up your upcoming Sunday with this vintage Sunshine Cake? It tastes great and is simple to prepare without much hassle.

Serves 6–8 | Prep. time 20 min. | Cooking time 50–60 min.

Ingredients
11 egg whites
6 egg yolks
1½ cups sugar
1 teaspoonful cream of tartar
1 cup flour
Grated peel of 1 orange

Directions

1. Beat the egg whites in a mixing bowl until they turn stiff and flaky. Add half the sugar.
2. Beat the yolks in another bowl. Add the remaining sugar and beat some more.
3. Combine the mixtures and then add the tartar, orange peel and flour.
4. Combine to make a smooth mixture.
5. Preheat the oven to 300°F. Grease a cake pan with cooking spray or melted butter.
6. Add the mixture to the pan and bake for 50–60 minutes, until evenly brown.

Jelly Roll

This was my absolute favorite when I was a little girl, and my kids love it too. It's the simplest recipe on a small bit of paper, but it works every time.

Serves 6 | Prep. time 15 min. | Cooking time 15 min

Ingredients

For the cake

3 eggs

1 cup water

2 teaspoons baking powder

1 cup sugar

1 cup flour

1 teaspoon vanilla

Pinch salt

¾ cup jam of your choice

<u>For dusting</u>
¼ cup icing sugar

Directions

1. Preheat the oven to 350°F and grease a 9x11 baking sheet.
2. Combine the ingredients and mix well. Spread them in the pan.
3. Bake 15 minutes, or until golden and cooked through.
4. Spread with jam and roll immediately. Dust with icing sugar.

Cheesy Strawberry Shortcakes

This recipe was my Dad's favorite dessert and my mom would make it for his birthday and father's day. I still can see his face light-up when she made it. It was her grandmother who made it when he was a child, so this recipe has been in our family for well over 80 years and it is such an easy dessert to make during strawberry picking season!

Serves 6 | Prep. time 25 min. | Cooking time 17 min

Ingredients
1 pint fresh strawberries, washed, stemmed, and sliced (any berries may be used)
1 1/2 cups all-purpose flour
2 teaspoons baking powder
1 teaspoon cinnamon
1/2 teaspoon salt

1/2 teaspoon baking soda
2 tablespoons cold unsalted butter, diced
1 1/2 cups shredded Monterey Jack cheese
1 cup sour cream
Whipping cream

Directions

1. Preheat oven to 425°F.
2. Sift together flour, baking powder, cinnamon, salt and soda into a mixing bowl. Add the butter and blend with a pastry tool until mixture forms coarse crumbs, about the size of peas. Stir in the cheese, then add sour cream. Stir until the mixture forms a soft dough.
3. Turn out the dough on a lightly floured surface and knead 6 times. Roll the dough out until 1/2 inch thick. Cut with a 3 ⅓-inch round cutter. Bake on ungreased baking sheet 15–17 minutes until golden brown. Cool on wire rack.
4. To assemble, cut cakes in half, add plenty of sliced strawberries, cover with the other cake's half. Arrange some more strawberry slices. Garnish with whipped cream and enjoy.

Green Angel Lime Cake

In this recipe from 1978, we combine a packaged cake mix with tart green Jell-O for a refreshingly different (and fun) dessert! Try it for St. Patrick's Day, or substitute your favorite colors and flavors.

Serves 10 | Prep. time 20 min. | Cooking time 40–45 min.

Ingredients
For the cake
1 package Angel Food cake mix*
2 (3-ounce) packages Lime Jell-O

For the icing
1 (3-ounce) package Lime Jell-O
1 cup boiling water

1 (9-ounce) package frozen whipped topping, thawed
Lime slice, coconut flakes for garnish, if desired

*other ingredients will be required, please check your package

Directions
1. Preheat the oven to 375°F and prepare an Angel cake or Bundt pan with a light coating of cooking spray.
2. In a mixing bowl, prepare the cake batter according to the package instructions.
3. Mix-in the Jell-O crystals only to incorporate.
4. Spoon the batter into the prepared pan.
5. Bake for 40–45 minutes, or until the cake springs back when pressed gently.
6. Remove the cake from the pan and let it cool completely.
7. To prepare the icing, combine the Jell-O with the boiling water and stir until it dissolves. Chill until it begins to thicken, and then fold it into the thawed whipped topping.
8. Frost the cake and garnish with lime slices, if desired.

Never-Fail Devil's Food Cake

This never-fail cake also never fails to surprise people with its simple yet delectable flavors. The time is right to get nostalgic with this chocolaty cake this weekend!

Serves 6–8 | Prep. time 10–20 min. | Cooking time 45 min.

Ingredients
½ cup butter, melted
2 cups brown sugar
2 ounces bitter (unsweetened) chocolate
½ cup milk
2 eggs, beaten
2½ cups flour
1 teaspoon vanilla extract
2 teaspoons baking powder

Directions

1. Preheat the oven to 350°F. Grease a cake pan (or two cake pans for layered cake) with cooking spray or melted butter and dust with flour (or line a cut parchment paper at the bottom of the pan).
2. Grate the chocolate.
3. Add the chocolate and 1½ cups of boiling water to a mixing bowl. Set aside to melt the chocolate.
4. Combine the butter and sugar in another bowl until the sugar dissolves. Add the eggs and combine.
5. Add the flour and baking powder. Add the milk little by little while continuing to stir the mixture.
6. Stir until you get a smooth mixture.
7. Add the chocolate and vanilla extract. Combine well.
8. Add the mixture to the pan and bake until evenly brown, about 40-45 minutes, when using only one pan. If using 2 pans, 30-35 minutes. To check if cooked, insert a toothpick in the middle of the cake, when ready it should come out clean. If not continue baking for a few more minutes until fully cooked.
9. Remove from oven and let cool on a wired rack. When completely cooled, unmold and frost if desired with your favorite frosting.

Note: for the frosting, my favorite is, using an electric mixer with the paddle attachment on, beat 1 stick of unsalted butter (½ cup) until creamy, add 2 ounces of melted semi-sweet baking chocolate, 1 ounce of strong coffee, and 1 teaspoon pure vanilla extract. Mix until well combined. Add, by ½ cup increments, 3-4 cups of powdered sugar. Beat after each increment at medium speed until the you have enough icing at the desired consistency. Spread evenly on the cake.

Peanut Butter Tandy Cake

The Tandy-Kake was a packaged cake that came out in the 1930s. It's been popular since then, and we can tell why! Here's how you can make them at home.

Serves 24 | Prep. time 25 min. | Cooking time 20 min.

Ingredients
4 eggs, room temperature
2 cups sugar
1 cup 2 % milk
1 teaspoon vanilla
2 cups flour
1 teaspoon baking powder
½ teaspoon salt

1 ¾ cups creamy peanut butter
½ cup icing sugar
⅓ cup heavy cream
1 cup semi-sweet chocolate chips

Directions
1. Preheat the oven to 350°F and coat a 10-inchx15-inchx1-inch baking sheet with cooking spray.
2. Combine the eggs and sugar and whisk until the sugar is completely dissolved and the mixture is thick and smooth.
3. Mix in the milk and vanilla.
4. In a separate bowl, combine the flour, baking powder, and salt. Stir the dry ingredients into the wet, and stir just until incorporated.
5. Spread the batter in the prepared pan and bake for 20–30 minutes. It's done when a toothpick inserted in the center comes out clean.
6. Let the cake cool for 20 minutes.
7. Stir the icing sugar into the peanut butter, and spread the mixture over the cake.
8. Heat the cream in a double boiler and stir in the chocolate chips. When the mixture is smooth, spread it over the peanut butter.
9. Refrigerate until set.

Kuchen

North Dakota serves an authentic recipe that originated with German settlers from the 1850s and has been passed down for generations. Kuchen is an amazingly comforting sweet dough cake, which is filled with fruit and custard. My mom makes hers with pears instead of apples, when in season.

Serves 6–8 | Prep. time 1 hour. | Cooking time 20 min

Ingredients
Kuchen base (2 pies)
2 large eggs
1½ cups sugar
1 teaspoon salt
2 cups warm milk
1 (1¼-ounce) package rapid rise yeast
6 cups all-purpose flour
½ cup oil

Vegetable oil for greasing

Fruit custard filling
4 cups heavy cream
6 eggs
1 cup sugar
Dash salt
4 apples, peeled, cored and sliced
2 teaspoons cinnamon
2 tablespoons sugar

Directions
1. To prepare the kuchen pie crusts, whisk the eggs, sugar and salt in a large bowl. Slowly add the warm milk and then mix in the flour and yeast.
2. Grease a clean large bowl generously with vegetable oil. Transfer the dough to this bowl, cover with plastic wrap, and set aside in a warm area so it can rise. It should double in size.
3. Preheat the oven to 350°F and grease a 9-inch baking pan.
4. To make the custard, add the eggs, sugar, heavy cream and salt to a heavy-bottomed saucepan. Whisk over medium heat until the custard thickens. Remove from heat.
5. Prepare the pie crust by lightly dusting a surface with flour and rolling out half the dough into a thick, round circle to fit in a 9-inch deep pie plate. Grease the pie plate with cooking spray. Place the dough in the pie plate. Repeat for the second pie.
6. Arrange the apple slices evenly on top of the dough of each pie.
7. Mix the cinnamon with 2 tablespoons of sugar. Sprinkle evenly over the apples. Pour half of the custard into each kuchen.
8. Place the kuchen in the oven and bake for 20 minutes. Remove from the oven and let cool down for at least 30 minutes before placing in the refrigerator until you are ready to serve.

Traditional Fruitcake

You may not have enjoyed this as a child, but we challenge you to give it another try as an adult. This recipe is the real (1930s) deal, and is best aged in rum. Hint: it's much easier to make than you think!

Serves 12 | Prep. time 20 min. | Cooking time 2 hours | Aging time 3–6 weeks

Ingredients
1 pound sultana raisins
2 cups mixed candied fruit, chopped
½ pound candied cherries
½ cup chopped walnuts
2 cups all-purpose flour
1 cup butter, softened

1 cup sugar
3 eggs
1 ½ teaspoons baking powder
1 teaspoon salt
¼ cup rum (or orange juice)
1 teaspoon rum extract

For aging, if desired
Cheesecloth
Rum

Directions

1. Heat the oven to 300°F and place a shallow pan of water on the bottom rack.
2. In a mixing bowl, combine the fruits and walnuts and coat them with half the flour.
3. In a separate bowl, beat the butter until creamy and add the sugar. Mix until light and fluffy, and then incorporate the eggs one at a time.
4. Add the remaining flour, baking powder, and salt.
5. Stir in the fruit, rum (or orange juice), and rum extract.
6. Prepare 12–inch a springform pan (or smaller pans of your choice) with 3 layers of waxed paper. Pour in the batter and bake over the pan of water for 2 hours.
7. When the cake is cooked, let it cool completely. Serve, or choose to age it with rum.
8. To age the cake, wrap it generously with cheesecloth and moisten the cheesecloth well with a rum-soaked brush. Wrap tightly in plastic and foil and refrigerate for 2–3 days. Repeat this process for up to 6 weeks or a minimum of 3 weeks, soaking it with more rum every 2–3 days and returning it to the fridge.

Plum Charlotte

I love this recipe for using up stale bread and fruit that might be past its peak. This was common in the 1940s, when people were very careful not to let anything go to waste. Feel free to substitute whatever fruit and bread you have.

Serves 4 | Prep. time 15 min. | Cooking time 45 min

Ingredients
8 slices white bread, torn or made into crumbs
1 pound plums, sliced (you can add in an apple, peach, or berries if you prefer)
½ cup sugar
1 teaspoon orange zest

¼ cup butter
1 cup orange juice

Directions
1. Butter a baking dish, and set the oven to 375°F.
2. Put a layer of bread in the bottom of the baking dish, and cover with a layer of fruit, a sprinkle of sugar, a bit of orange zest, and a few dots of butter.
3. Repeat the layers until the ingredients are all used, finishing with bread and butter.
4. Pour the orange juice over, and bake for 45 minutes, or until the edges are bubbly and the top is golden.

Molasses Stack Cake

For special occasions, this vintage Molasses stack cake is one special food. Back in time, Pioneer weddings were incomplete without celebrating with this classic cake. It was one of the most preferred welcome recipe for special guests and this cake has never failed to make a lasting delicious impression.

Serves 4 | Prep. time 20 min. | Cooking time 20 min.

Ingredients
1 large egg
1 cup molasses
½ cup buttermilk
½ cup shortening or butter, melted
½ teaspoon baking powder
4 cups all-purpose flour

1-2 cups apple butter
½ teaspoon cinnamon
¼ teaspoon nutmeg

Directions
1. Preheat an oven to 350⁰F.
2. In a bowl (preferably medium-large size), combine the butter, buttermilk, egg, baking powder and molasses.
3. Add the nutmeg and cinnamon on top. Combine well.
4. Add the flour and combine again until no lumps.
5. Roll the mixture into a thin layer of ½-inch thick.
6. Cut out circles from it and place over a greased baking sheet.
7. Bake for about 15-20 minutes.
8. Cool down and spread some apple butter between each stack before serving.

Pecan Sticky Buns

We are pleased to share this old family recipe, which takes a little effort but is well worth it. When you eat these buns, keep in mind that life on a farm was a lot more active than life at a desk, and adjust accordingly!

Serves 12 | Prep. time 30 min. | Resting time 1 hour | Cooking time 30 min.

Ingredients

For the dough

1 cup whole milk

¼ cup sugar

1 tablespoon yeast

1 teaspoon salt

2 eggs, lightly beaten

3 ½ cups flour

¼ cup melted shortening (not oil)

For the topping

¼ cup butter

1 cup brown sugar

½ cup light corn syrup

1 cup chopped pecans

For the cinnamon filling

3 tablespoons salted butter, melted

1 cup brown sugar

2 tablespoons cinnamon

Directions

1. In a Dutch oven over medium heat, warm the milk until it is warm to touch but not steaming. Remove it from the burner.
2. Stir in the sugar and yeast and let it sit until the yeast blooms and is fragrant.
3. Add the salt, eggs, and half the flour. Mix well for 2–3 minutes.
4. Add the melted shortening and the remaining flour. Turn the dough out onto a floured surface and knead for another 5 minutes.
5. Place the dough back into the warm Dutch oven and cover it with the lid. Let it rise for 30 minutes or until doubled in size.
6. Meanwhile, prepare the pecan sauce. In a saucepan over medium-low heat, warm the butter, sugar, and corn syrup, stirring often. When the sugar is melted, remove the pot from the heat, and do not let the mixture get too hot. Set it aside.
7. Butter a 9x13 pan and pour the caramel in. Spread the pecans over the caramel.

8. Turn the risen dough out onto a piece of parchment, and roll it out into a rectangle about 12x24 inches. Brush the dough with melted butter and sprinkle on the sugar and cinnamon.

9. Starting on the short end, roll it up as tightly as you can and pinch the edge. Cut it into 12 equal pieces and arrange them, evenly spaced, on the topping.

10. Cover with a damp towel and let them rise for 30 minutes.

11. Preheat the oven to 375°F, and when it's hot, bake the rolls for 30 minutes. Cover them with foil if they start to get too brown.

12. Remove the pan from the oven and let it sit for 5 minutes.

13. Set out a tray or dish that is slightly larger than your baking pan. Carefully tip the rolls onto the platter. (Place the platter upside down on the baking pan, and flip them over together.)

14. Serve warm.

CUSTARDS, PUDDINGS, AND PASTRIES

Steamed Chocolate Pudding

Steaming pudding is a lost art; nowadays we default to "Sauce 'n Cake" packets. We're here to put a stop to that. My mother used to make this pudding, which was copied out of a Betty Crocker book sometime in the 1950s and adjusted to her taste.

Serves 8 | Prep. time 15 min. | Cooking time 2 hours

Ingredients

For the pudding

1 egg
1 cup sugar
2 tablespoons butter, softened
2 squares unsweetened chocolate, melted
1 ¾ cups sifted all-purpose flour
1 teaspoon salt
¼ teaspoon cream of tartar
¼ teaspoon baking soda
1 cup milk

For the sauce

¾ cup icing sugar
¼ cup unsweetened cocoa powder
¼ cup heavy cream
½ teaspoon vanilla

Directions

1. Prepare a steamer: you will need a 1-quart mold or heatproof individual bowls that fits inside a Dutch oven, and a heatproof colander to keep it off the bottom of the pot. Place the colander inside the Dutch oven and add 2 inches of water. Place the pot over medium-high heat and bring the water to a simmer.
2. In a mixing bowl, beat the egg, sugar, butter, and melted chocolate until well combined.
3. In a separate bowl, combine the salt, cream of tartar, and baking soda.
4. To the chocolate mixture, add the dry ingredients in batches alternating with the milk.
5. Pour the batter into the mold and place it inside the colander in the pot. Place a piece of waxed paper over the pudding to prevent water droplets landing in the pudding.
6. Place the mold into the colander and cover the pot with a lid. Cook over low heat for 2 hours, checking halfway through to make sure the water is at a low simmer and adding more if necessary.

Raspberry Custard Kuchen

With this old German dessert, you can have your cake and your pudding. When we were growing up, there was a German family just down the road. We had such lovely baked things in their kitchen, and this was one of those things. Substitute any fruits or berries that are in season.

Serves 10 | Prep. time 20 min. | Cooking time 40 min.

Ingredients
1 ½ cups all-purpose flour, divided
1 teaspoon salt
½ cup cold butter
2 tablespoons heavy whipping cream
½ cup sugar

101

<u>For the filling</u>
3 cups fresh raspberries
1 cup sugar
1 tablespoon all-purpose flour
2 large eggs, beaten
1 cup heavy whipping cream
1 teaspoon vanilla extract

Directions

1. Preheat the oven to 375°F, and prepare a 9x13 baking dish with butter or cooking spray.
2. In a mixing bowl, combine 1 cup of flour with the salt. Cut in the butter until crumbly. Stir in the cream, and pat the base into the prepared pan.
3. Combine the half cup sugar with the remaining flour and sprinkle them over the crust. Arrange the berries on top.
4. In a large bowl, combine the cup of sugar with the tablespoon of flour. Beat in the eggs, cream, and vanilla. Pour the custard over the berries.
5. Bake for 40–45 minutes until the custard is set and lightly browned. Serve warm or chilled.

Vintage Plum Pudding

This was one of my favorite desserts as a child. Unlike these, ours was made in tin cans. We sliced it thick, steamed it over boiling water, and served it with a generous helping of hard sauce.

Serves 6-8 | Prep. time 30 min. | Cooking time 20 min.

Ingredients
¼ cup unsalted butter, softened, divided
2 eggs
¼ cup brandy
1 granny smith apple, peeled, cored, and diced
½ cup dried currants
¼ cup raisins
¼ cup chopped pecans

⅓ cup brown sugar
1 cup fresh breadcrumbs
¾ teaspoon ground cinnamon
Pinch ground cloves
Pinch ground allspice
Pinch ground nutmeg

For the brandy syrup
½ cup sugar
1 ¼ cups brandy

For the hard sauce
¼ cup butter, softened
¾ cup icing sugar
½ teaspoon vanilla extract
1 tablespoon dark rum

Directions
1. Use 1 tablespoon of the butter to grease the ramekins.
2. Cut eight 3-inch squares of foil and use 1 tablespoon of butter to grease those on one side.
3. Place a large pot (big enough to fit all the ramekins) on the stove, and boil a kettle of water.
4. In a medium mixing bowl, beat the eggs with the brandy until smooth. Add the apples, currants, raisins, pecans, sugar, breadcrumbs, cinnamon, cloves, allspice, and nutmeg. Mix well.
5. Divide the pudding batter between the ramekins and cover them with the foil, buttered side down. If necessary, you can tie the foil with string.
6. Arrange the ramekins in the pot and pour boiling water in around them until the water comes halfway up the sides of the dishes.

7. Place the pot over medium heat and cook for 15–20 minutes, or until a toothpick inserted in the middle of a pudding comes out clean.

8. Meanwhile, prepare the syrup. Combine the sugar and the brandy in a small saucepan and bring it to a simmer. Cook for about 5 minutes, until the sugar is fully dissolved and the mixture is syrupy.

9. Make the hard sauce. Combine the butter, sugar, and vanilla and beat until fluffy, about 1 minute. Gradually incorporate the rum.

10. To serve, tip each pudding onto a dish and pour a few spoonfuls of brandy syrup over them. Top with some hard sauce, and serve!

Old-Fashioned Plum Pudding

We used to have this every Christmas, but it's been years since I've seen it. I was glad to find this handwritten recipe of my aunt's, because I would like to continue the tradition. We made it in cans and cut thick slices to steam over boiling water and serve with hard sauce.

NOTE! She writes that it's a very old recipe, and you use a coffee cup to measure these things, not a teacup. (I think this is probably close to a measuring cup, and not the large mugs we use today.) I just love the imprecision of it. Women who made this probably learned it from their mothers, going by habit, instinct, memory, and observation.

Serves 4 | Prep. time 30 min. | Cooking time 4 hours | Aging time 1 month

Ingredients

1 cup suet
1 cup bread crumbs
½ pound citron
3 cups flour
1 teaspoon baking soda
1 teaspoon baking powder
2 teaspoons cinnamon
½ teaspoon ground ginger
½ teaspoon ground cloves
½ teaspoon salt, or to taste
1 pound currants
2 pounds raisins
½ cup chopped walnuts
4 eggs, lightly beaten
1 cup dark brown sugar
1 cup molasses
1 cup milk
1 cup apple jelly

Hard sauce
2 tablespoons butter
2 tablespoons flour
½ cup brown sugar
1 cup boiling water
½ teaspoon salt
1 teaspoon vanilla
2 tablespoons rum, or to taste

Directions

1. Grind the suet, bread, and citron through a meat grinder (or pulse a few times in a food processor).
2. In a separate bowl, combine the flour, baking soda, baking powder, spices, and salt.
3. Separately, combine the currants, raisins, and walnuts. Take one cup of the flour mixture and dredge the fruit with it.
4. Beat together the eggs, brown sugar, molasses, milk, and apple jelly, and then fold everything together until combined.
5. Ladle the batter into molds or cans, and steam for 4 hours.
6. The pudding keeps well and is best if you let it sit a month. Serve with hard sauce.
7. To make the hard sauce, melt the butter in a medium saucepan, and whisk in the flour until smooth. Cook for a minute or so.
8. Mix in the brown sugar and boiling water, and cook over medium heat until it thickens to your liking.
9. Stir in the salt, vanilla, and rum.

Delmonaco's Restaurant Pudding

The first Delmonaco's Restaurant opened in 1827 in New York City. The family eventually sold the company in 1919, but this recipe has been rescued from the clutches of time. With its common ingredients and simple preparation, we think it deserves a comeback!

Serves 6 | Prep. time 30 min. | Cooking time 30 min.

Ingredients
5 egg yolks
6 tablespoons sugar
1 quart milk
3 tablespoons cornstarch
½ teaspoon salt
1 (14-ounce) can peaches, ½ cup of the syrup reserved

<u>For the meringue</u>
5 egg whites
2 tablespoons sugar

Directions

1. Lightly butter a 2-quart casserole dish and preheat the oven to 325°F.
2. Beat the egg yolks until they are light, and then gradually add the sugar and corn starch.
3. Pour the milk into a saucepan and warm it up. When it is no longer cold, whisk in the egg mixture, salt, and peach syrup. Heat and stir until it is well thickened.
4. Pour the custard into the prepared dish, and bake until it is set enough to hold the next layers.
5. Drain the peaches and layer them on the custard.
6. Beat the eggs until stiff, and gradually incorporate the sugar. Spoon the topping over the peaches and bake until golden.

Magic Caramel Pudding

It doesn't get much easier than this delectable vintage pudding from 1930! And the caramel deep flavors are surprisingly delicious.

Serves 2–4 per can | Prep. time 3 min. |
Cooking time 3 hours | Chilling time 12 hours

Ingredients
1–3 cans Eagle Brand sweetened condensed milk

Directions

1. Place the can or cans of condensed milk in a pot of boiling water. The water should be deep enough to cover the cans.
2. Keep the water at the boiling point for three hours.
3. Carefully drain the water and cool the can(s). Refrigerate overnight.
4. To serve, warm the can in a bowl of hot water for one minute. Poke a hole in the bottom of the can, and then open the top with a can opener.
5. Heat a butter knife under warm water and run it around the edge of the pan to loosen the pudding. Reheat the knife before slicing the pudding.

Old-Fashioned Strawberry Fluff

In 1929, Minute Tapioca Co. published this classic strawberry fluff recipe in their popular book *A Cook's Tour with Minute Tapioca*. Tapioca is a starch extracted from the cassava root. Portuguese and Spanish explorers carried the cassava plant to Africa, Asia and the West Indies; from there it spread throughout South America.

Serves 6 | Prep. time 10–15 min. | Cooking time 15 min.

Ingredients

3 tablespoons Minute Tapioca
⅛ teaspoon salt
1 cup sugar (divided)
1 quart fresh strawberries, hulled (divided)
1 egg white, stiffly beaten

Directions

1. Add ¾ cup of the sugar and half of the strawberries to a mixing bowl. Set aside for 15–20 minutes.
2. Crush the mixture; reserve the juice.
3. Add the pulp to the upper part of a double boiler.
4. Add water to make about 2½ cups of liquid.
5. Add the tapioca and salt; stir and then cook until the tapioca is clear, about 15 minutes.
6. Let cool.
7. Halve the remaining strawberries and top them with the remaining sugar.
8. Combine the beaten egg white and the berry mixture with the tapioca mixture.
9. Top with some whole strawberries and whipped cream (optional).

Rhubarb Radio Pudding

When I was little, I always wanted to know why this dessert was called radio pudding. Apparently, the recipe came from a radio broadcast many years ago.

Serves 6 | Prep. time 15 min. | Cooking time 35 min.

Ingredients
1 cup all-purpose flour
⅓ cup sugar
1 ½ teaspoons baking powder
½ teaspoon baking soda
½ teaspoon salt
1 ½ cups rhubarb, diced (if frozen, drain excess liquid)

½ cup milk

1 egg

½ teaspoon vanilla extract

For the sauce

1 cup boiling water

¼ cup brown sugar, packed

¼ cup butter

1 tablespoon lemon juice

1 teaspoon lemon zest, grated

Directions

1. Preheat the oven to 350°F and butter an 8-inch square baking dish.
2. To make the pudding, whisk together the flour, sugar, baking powder, baking soda, and salt.
3. Toss the rhubarb in the dry ingredients.
4. Beat the milk, egg, and vanilla together until combined, and then stir them into the dry ingredients just until combined.
5. Spoon the pudding mixture into the prepared baking dish.
6. In a heatproof bowl, combine the boiling water, brown sugar, and butter until the sugar dissolves and the butter melts. Stir in the lemon juice and lemon zest.
7. Pour the hot water mixture over the pudding and bake for 30–35 minutes, until the top is golden and a knife inserted in the center comes out clean.

1950s Magic Jello® Dessert

This is how nostalgia tastes! It's easy and tasty, and you'll wonder why you haven't made it all these years.

Serves 6 | Prep. time 30 min. | Chilling time 14-16 hours

Ingredients
1 package (4 serving size) lime Jell-O
1 package (4 serving size) orange Jell-O
1 package (4 serving size) strawberry Jell-O
1 package (4 serving size) lemon Jell-O
3 cups boiling water
1 1/2 cup cold water
1 cup boiling water

1/2 cup cold water

1 (8-ounce) container Cool Whip®, thawed

Directions

1. Prepare the lime, orange, and strawberry Jell-O separately, according to the package instructions. Pour each into an 8-inch square glass pan, and chill.
2. When they have set, use a warm knife to slice them into ½-inch cubes. You'll use 1 ½ cups of each.
3. Pour the lemon Jell-O powder into a heatproof bowl and add 1 cup of boiling water. When the Jell-O has dissolved, stir in half a cup of cool water. Refrigerate for 45 minutes or so, until the mixture is gelatinous (like uncooked egg white) but not set.
4. Stir in half the Cool Whip, and then the gelatin cubes.
5. Spread the mixture in a 9x5 loaf pan and refrigerate overnight.
6. Serve with the remaining Cool Whip, garnished with the remaining leftover cubes if desired.

1920s Rice Pudding

Oh, the wholesome simplicity of this pudding just makes my heart swell. I like it warm but chill yours if you prefer that. I was taught to make something like this when the oven is on anyway, such as when you're roasting a turkey.

Serves 4 | Prep. time 15 min. | Cooking time 3 hours

Ingredients
5 tablespoons long grain rice (dry)
1 quart whole milk
½ cup cane syrup
½ teaspoon salt
½ teaspoon ground cinnamon
Pinch ground nutmeg
½ cup raisins

Directions
1. Grease a casserole dish.
2. Combine all the ingredients and pour them into the dish.
3. Cook on the stovetop at low heat for 3 hours, stirring often.

Raspberry Halo Mold

This is how nostalgia tastes! It's easy and tasty, and you'll wonder why you haven't made it all these years.

Serves 6 | Prep. time 30 min. plus chilling time

Ingredients
1 (15-ounce) package raspberries, thawed
2 (3-ounce) packages raspberry gelatin
3 cups boiling water
4 cups mini marshmallows
1 cup heavy cream, whipped
1 (14-ounce) angel food cake, cut in ½-inch cubes

Directions

1. Prepare a 10-inch cake mold with a light coating of
2. Ensure that the raspberries are completely thawed, and set aside any juices.
3. Dissolve the gelatin and 3 cups of the mini marshmallows in the boiling water, and stir in the reserved syrup.
4. Chill until it is almost thickened, and then whip until it is foamy.
5. Add the raspberries, whipped cream, cake, and the remaining mini marshmallows.
6. Pour the mixture into the prepared mold and chill until firm.

1920s Cream Puffs

We modern folks did not create the glorious thing that is the cream puff, so please enjoy this tasty relic of days gone by.

Serves 10 | Prep. time 25 min. | Cooking time 35 min.

Ingredients
1 cup water
½ cup butter
½ teaspoon salt
1 cup all-purpose flour
4 large eggs
2 tablespoons milk
1 egg yolk, lightly beaten
2 cups heavy whipping cream
⅓ cup icing sugar

1 teaspoon vanilla extract
Additional icing sugar for dusting

Directions

1. In a large saucepan, heat the water, butter, and salt until boiling. Add the flour in one addition and stir quickly with a sturdy wooden spoon until smooth. Set it aside for 5 minutes to cool.
2. One at a time, mix in the eggs. Beat until the batter is smooth and shiny.
3. Preheat the oven to 400°F, and mix the milk with the egg yolk to make an egg wash.
4. Measure out ¼ cupfuls and place them on a baking sheet. Brush them with the egg mixture. Bake for 30–35 minutes, or until golden brown. Cut a small slit in the top for steam and remove them to cooling racks.
5. In a clean bowl, beat the cream until it begins to thicken. Gradually add the icing sugar and vanilla, and continue mixing until thick.
6. Slice the cream puffs and scoop out some of the soft dough inside. Fill with cream, and dust with icing sugar.

COOKIES, SQUARES, AND DOUGHNUTS

Pineapple Cheesecake Squares

This is my aunt's adaptation of an old Eagle Brand recipe from 1956. It can certainly be made as a pie, but it was intended to be cut into squares.

Serves 9 | Prep. time 20 min. | Cooking time 35 min.

Ingredients
20 graham crackers, finely crushed
¼ cup butter, melted

6 ounces cream cheese, softened

1 (15 oz.) can Eagle Brand® Sweetened Condensed Milk

2 eggs, separated

3 tablespoons sugar

1 teaspoon vanilla

2 tablespoons cornstarch

1 ½ cups canned crushed pineapple with juice

1 tablespoon lemon juice

8-10 maraschino cherries, minced and drained or ⅓ cup dried cherries, minced

Directions

1. Preheat the oven to 350°F.
2. Combine the crushed graham cracker crumbs with the butter and press the mixture into an 8-inch square baking pan.
3. Beat the cream cheese until creamy and mix in the Eagle Brand and egg yolks.
4. Beat the egg whites until foamy and gradually incorporate the sugar.
5. Fold the egg whites and vanilla into the cream cheese mixture, and spoon the batter over the graham crust. Bake for 35 minutes, and then cool completely.
6. Meanwhile, in a saucepan, combine the cornstarch, pineapple, and lemon juice. Bring it to a simmer and cook for 10 minutes, and then set the sauce aside to cool for a few minutes.
7. Spread the sauce over the cheesecake layer and sprinkle the cherries on top.

Strawberry Kisses

My husband bought a bottle of Nestlé strawberry milk syrup, which my kids absolutely detested. I was looking through some old recipes and came across this gem from 1962. Problem solved!

Makes 40 cookies | Prep. time 10 min. |
Cooking time 15 min. (per tray)

Ingredients
3 egg whites
¾ cup sugar
¼ cup Nestlé Strawberry Quik®
⅓ cup crushed soda crackers

1 teaspoon grated lemon rind
Coarse sugar for dusting

Directions
1. Preheat the oven to 350°F.
2. Beat the egg whites until stiff, and gradually incorporate the sugar and the syrup until stiff, glossy peaks form.
3. Fold in the crackers and the lemon zest.
4. Drop by spoonfuls onto greased cookie sheets, sprinkle lightly with coarse sugar, and bake for 15 minutes.

Fudge Squares

The only identification on this recipe said that it came from Chatelaine. From the condition of the paper I'd say it was either a well-loved recipe, or it came from sometimes in the 1600s.

Serves 12 | Prep. time 10 min. | Cooking time 30 min.

Ingredients
2 squares unsweetened chocolate
¾ cup sifted pastry flour
½ teaspoon baking powder
¼ teaspoon salt
⅓ cup vegetable shortening
1 cup sugar
1 teaspoon vanilla
2 eggs

⅓ cup dates, finely chopped
⅓ cup walnuts

Directions

1. Preheat the oven to 350°F and coat an 8-inch square baking pan with butter or cooking spray.
2. Melt the chocolate in a double boiler.
3. Sift the flour with the baking powder and salt.
4. In a separate bowl, beat the shortening with the melted chocolate. Gradually add the sugar and vanilla.
5. Add the eggs and beat until fluffy. Stir in the flour, dates, and walnuts.
6. Bake for about 30 minutes, or until the squares start to pull away from the edges of the pan.

WWII Carrot Cookies

Who needs a muffin or a cake, when you can have all the goodness of carrot cake and cream cheese icing in a cookie? This 1930s recipe has everything you're craving.

Makes 36 cookies | Prep. time 25 min. |
Cooking time 12 min. (per tray)

Ingredients
1 cup sliced cooked carrots, drained and mashed
¾ cup unsalted butter
¾ cup sugar

¾ cup light brown sugar

1 egg

1 ½ teaspoons vanilla

2 cups flour

2 teaspoons baking powder

½ teaspoon salt

½ teaspoon grated ginger

1 teaspoon cinnamon

1 cup chopped walnuts

<u>Cream Cheese Frosting</u>

8 ounces cream cheese, at room temperature

½ cup unsalted butter, at room temperature

1 teaspoon vanilla

3 ½ cups icing sugar

Directions

1. Preheat the oven to 375°F and line two baking sheets with parchment.
2. Cream the butter with the sugars until fluffy. Beat in the egg and vanilla.
3. With the mixer on low, add the carrots.
4. Mix in the dry ingredients, ginger, and walnuts.
5. Form the cookies by dropping them in 2-tablespoon scoops on the prepared sheets 2 inches apart.
6. Bake for 11–12 minutes, until firm but not browned. Let them cool on the sheets for a few minutes and then transfer them to a cooling rack.
7. Meanwhile, make the icing. Whip the cream cheese and butter until light, and then beat in the vanilla and icing sugar.
8. Frost the cookies when they're completely cool.

Divinity

This is a candy I'd only read about in books, so I was delighted to come across a recipe for it in *the Neighborhood Cook Book* when we were cleaning out a cupboard. This recipe is from 1914.

Serves 12 | Prep. time 10 min. | Cooking time 15 min

Ingredients
3 cups sugar
1 cup corn syrup
¾ cup water
3 egg whites
2 cups chopped walnuts or pecans
1 tablespoon vanilla

Directions
1. Line a baking sheet with parchment paper.
2. Place the egg whites in a bowl and beat with an electric mixer until stiff peaks form and set aside.
3. Combine the sugar, corn syrup and water in a large saucepan and cook over medium-high heat.

4. Stir constantly while cooking until the liquid reaches approximately 260°F on a candy thermometer. If you do not have a candy thermometer, a drop of the mixture put into a glass of icy cold water will form a ball and hold its shape.
5. Remove the saucepan from the heat and slowly start to drizzle the syrup into the egg whites while beating on high.
6. Add the vanilla and continue beating on high until the candy takes on a glossy appearance.
7. Quickly stir in the nuts and drop by rounded spoonfuls onto the baking sheet.
8. Set aside and allow to cool and harden slightly before serving.

Date and Nut Squares

This recipe showed up in a 1917 *Good Housekeeping* magazine. These are chewy and nutritious!

Serves 12 | Prep. time 10 min. | Cooking time 30 min.

Ingredients
¾ cup all-purpose flour
1 cup sugar
1 teaspoon baking powder
1 cup chopped dates
¼ teaspoon salt
1 cup chopped pecans or walnuts

2 eggs
Icing sugar (for dusting)

Directions
1. Preheat the oven to 350°F and coat an 8-inch square baking pan with butter or cooking spray.
2. In a large bowl, combine the flour, sugar, baking powder, dates, salt, nuts, and eggs.
3. Spread the mixture in the prepared pan and bake for 30–35 minutes, or until a knife inserted in the center comes out clean.
4. Cool the squares and dust them with icing sugar before serving.

Whoopie Pies

Whoopie pies are a popular Pennsylvania Amish tradition and also a New England phenomenon. They're a real comfort food often enjoyed with a glass of milk. This vintage pie dates back to 1925, when Labadie's Bakery in Lewiston, Maine, started selling it soon after it opened. A fluffy white filling makes this pie creamier than ever. The dark brown crust is made from soft cookies. As per Amish legend, this pie got its name because children used to cheer "whoopee!" whenever they found it in their lunch bags.

Serves 8 | Prep. time 30 min. | Cooking time 60 min.

Ingredients
1¼ teaspoons baking soda
1 teaspoon salt
2 cups all-purpose flour

½ cup cocoa powder
1 cup buttermilk
½ cup (1 stick) unsalted butter, softened
1 teaspoon vanilla
1 large egg
1 cup packed brown sugar

Filling
½ cup (1 stick) unsalted butter, softened
2 cups marshmallow cream
1¼ cups confectioners' sugar
1 teaspoon vanilla

Directions

1. Preheat the oven to 350°F. Grease two baking sheets with cooking spray or melted butter.
2. Whisk the flour, cocoa, baking soda and salt in a medium-large bowl.
3. Combine the buttermilk and vanilla in another bowl.
4. Beat the butter and brown sugar in a third bowl until the sugar dissolves.
5. Add the eggs and combine well.
6. Alternately add the buttermilk and flour mixture in batches, mixing continuously until you get a smooth mixture.
7. Place ¼-cup mounds of the mixture on the baking sheets, keeping a 2-inch interval between them.
8. Bake both sheets simultaneously, one above the other, for about 12 minutes or until the tops of the pies are puffed, switching the top and bottom sheets halfway through.
9. Let cool completely.
10. Prepare the filling by whisking the filling ingredients in a mixing bowl for 2–3 minutes.
11. Arrange half of the prepared cakes, spread the filling over them, and top with the remaining cakes.

Forgotten Cookies

These are called forgotten cookies because they sit in the oven all night. Try them!

Makes 48 cookies | Prep. time 15 min. | Cooking time 10 hours

Ingredients
2 egg whites
Pinch of salt
¾ cup sugar
½ teaspoon vanilla
6 ounces mini chocolate chips
1 cup chopped pecans

Directions

1. Preheat the oven to 350°F and cover 2 baking sheets with foil.
2. Beat the egg whites with the salt, and gradually add the sugar. Beat until stiff.
3. Gently mix in the other ingredients, being careful not to deflate the meringue.
4. Drop in small spoonfuls onto the sheets. Turn off the oven, and place the trays inside.
5. The next morning, take the trays out of the oven and transfer the cookies to an airtight container.

Date Pinwheel Cookies

These pretty cookies are going to transport you to the past! We would often see these at bake sales and church picnics, and I was always attracted to the swirl pattern. I love to make them now.

Makes 30 cookies | Prep. time 30 min. | Chilling time 2 hours | Cooking time 12 min. (per tray)

Ingredients

½ cup butter softened

½ cup brown sugar

1 teaspoon vanilla extract

1 egg

2 cups all-purpose flour
¼ teaspoon salt
¼ teaspoon baking soda
1 cup chopped fresh dates
¾ cup sugar, divided
½ cup water
1 cup chopped pecans or walnuts

Directions

1. Beat the butter and brown sugar until light and fluffy. Mix in the vanilla and egg.
2. Add the flour, salt, and baking soda. Mix well until the dough comes together, and then wrap it in plastic and refrigerate for an hour.
3. Prepare the date filling. Combine the dates, ¼ cup of sugar, and the water in a small saucepan over medium heat. Bring it to a boil and simmer for five minutes, stirring and breaking up the dates with the spoon. When the mixture is a thick paste, remove it from the heat and let it cool. Stir in the nuts.
4. Lay out a sheet of parchment and flour it lightly.
5. Roll out the dough into a 12x8-inch rectangle. Spread the cooled filling on the dough, leaving a half-inch border.
6. Using the parchment to help, roll the dough from the long side. Wrap and refrigerate at least a few hours, or overnight.
7. Preheat the oven to 375°F and prepare 2 cookie sheets with parchment paper.
8. Unwrap the dough roll and slice the cookies into ½-inch rounds. Arrange them on the cookie sheets and bake for 10–12 minutes.

1945 Chocolate Honey Crisps

This recipe came from a 1945 Crisco® Cookbook.

Makes 24 cookies | Prep. time 15 min. |
Cooking time 12–15 min. (per tray)

Ingredients
½ cup Crisco shortening

⅓ cup honey

1 egg

3 tablespoons milk

1 cup flour

½ teaspoon salt

1 teaspoon baking powder

½ teaspoon cinnamon

½ teaspoon cloves

1 cup semi-sweet chocolate chips
½ cup chopped nuts

Directions
1. Preheat the oven to 375°F and grease two cookie sheets.
2. Cream the Crisco with the honey until it is well incorporated, and then add the egg.
3. Add the milk and sift in the dry ingredients. Mix well.
4. Fold in the chocolate chips and the nuts.
5. Drop the dough in spoonfuls onto the prepared sheets. Bake for 12–15 minutes, until the edges are browned.

Snickerdoodles

These cookies might be familiar to you, but it places them in a different light to realize that people have been eating them for over a hundred years. They likely originated in New England.

Serves 6-8 | Prep. time 25 min. | Cooking time 10 min.

Ingredients
1 ½ cups sugar
½ cup butter
½ cup shortening
2 eggs
1 teaspoon vanilla
2 ¾ cups all-purpose flour
1 ½ teaspoons cream of tartar
1 teaspoon baking soda
½ teaspoon salt

Cinnamon sugar
2 tablespoons sugar
2–3 teaspoons cinnamon

Directions

1. Preheat the oven to 400°F.
2. In a large mixing bowl, beat the sugar, butter, and shortening until light and fluffy.
3. Add the eggs and vanilla, and mix well.
4. Add the flour, cream of tartar, baking soda, and salt, and stir until the dough is uniform.
5. Make the cinnamon sugar. Take scoops of the cookie dough, roll them in balls, and roll the balls in the dough.
6. Bake on cookie sheets for 8–10 minutes, just until set. Transfer to a rack right away, and cool.

Chocolate Chip Oat Cookies

Here's one for the ages! It seems some things haven't changed much – this recipe goes all the way back to the 1930s, where it appeared on a cereal box. (Raisins optional, cranberries are good too.) If you have little ones, this recipe is nice to use because they're not too sweet.

Serves 12 | Prep. time 15 min. | Cooking time 10 min

Ingredients
1 cup packed brown sugar
2 large eggs
½ cup whole milk
¾ cup vegetable oil
1 teaspoon vanilla extract
2 cups all-purpose flour

1 teaspoon baking soda

1 teaspoon salt

1 teaspoon ground cinnamon

1 teaspoon ground nutmeg

2 cups old-fashioned oats

½ cup semisweet chocolate chips

½ cup raisins

Directions

1. In a large mixing bowl, combine the sugar, eggs, milk, oil, and vanilla.
2. Sift in the flour, baking soda, salt, cinnamon, and nutmeg. Mix well.
3. Add the oats, chocolate chips, and raisins, and let it sit for 10–15 minutes.
4. Heat the oven to 350°F.
5. Drop the batter by the spoonful onto ungreased baking sheets, and bake for 10 minutes, or until golden around the edges.

Wisconsin Jelly-Filled Cookies

These cookies are both attractive and fun to make. The recipe comes from a 1964 cookbook published by the Wisconsin Department of Agriculture to encourage people to use dairy products. As if we needed our arms twisted!

Makes 24 cookies | Prep. time 15 min. |
Cooking time 8–10 min. per tray

Ingredients
3 ½ cups sifted cake flour
2 teaspoons baking powder
½ teaspoon salt
½ cup butter
1 cup sugar
2 eggs, beaten

2 tablespoons heavy cream
1 tablespoon vanilla extract
Icing sugar, for dusting
Tart red jelly or jam

Directions
1. Preheat the oven to 375°F and grease 2 cookie sheets.
2. In a mixing bowl, sift together the flour, baking powder, and salt.
3. In a separate bowl, beat the butter with the sugar until light and fluffy. Add the eggs, cream, and vanilla.
4. Add the dry ingredients and mix well. Form the dough into a disk, wrap, and chill for 3 hours.
5. Sprinkle a work surface with icing sugar and split the dough in half and roll it out to a quarter of an inch thick. Use a doughnut cutter to cut shapes, and arrange them on a prepared cookie sheet.
6. Roll out the second batch of dough. Using a plain round cookie cutter (the same diameter as your other one) cut a second batch of cookies and place them on the other tray.
7. Bake the cookies for 8–10 minutes, or until they are lightly browned.
8. When they are completely cool, dust the cookies with icing sugar. Spread jelly on the plain cookies and top with the doughnut-shaped ones.

Spicy Ginger Bran Cookies

I found a magazine page folded in a recipe box: a 1982 recipe for Kellogg's Bran Flakes® crackle cookies. One of the ingredients will raise your eyebrows, but I thought it was worth a try. They're delicious!

Makes 48 cookies | Prep. time 30 min. | Chilling time 1 hour | Cooking time 12–15 min. (per tray)

Ingredients
2 ½ cups all-purpose flour
1 cup 40% Bran Flakes cereal
2 teaspoons baking powder
½ teaspoon ground cinnamon
½ teaspoon ground cloves
¼ teaspoon ground nutmeg

¼ teaspoon ground ginger

1 ½ cups sugar

½ cup mayonnaise

2 eggs

2 teaspoons vanilla

¼ cup icing sugar

Directions

1. In a mixing bowl, combine the dry ingredients.
2. In a separate bowl, beat the sugar with the mayonnaise until fluffy. Add the eggs one at a time and mix them in, together with the vanilla.
3. Fold in the dry ingredients and mix to incorporate. Refrigerate for 1 hour.
4. Preheat the oven to 350°F and grease two cookie sheets.
5. Using buttered hands, roll the dough into 1 ½-inch balls. Coat them with icing sugar and arrange them 2 inches apart on the prepared cookie sheets.
6. Bake for 12–15 minutes, until they are lightly browned and set around the edges.

Pistachio Cream Cheese Refrigerator Cookies

Are you looking for something different that you're sure people will love? Look no further than this vintage recipe.

Makes 48 cookies | Prep. time 30 min. | Chilling time 1 hour | Cooking time 7–9 min. (per tray)

Ingredients

½ cup butter, softened

3 ounces cream cheese, softened

1 egg

1 ½ cups icing sugar

3 teaspoons grated lemon zest

1 teaspoon vanilla extract

2-4 drops green food coloring

2 ½ cups all-purpose flour

½ teaspoon baking powder

½ teaspoon salt

½ cup finely chopped pistachios

60 shelled pistachios (about 1/3 cup)

Directions

1. In a mixing bowl, combine the butter and cream cheese until they are light and fluffy.
2. Beat in the egg, icing sugar, lemon zest, vanilla, and food coloring.
3. In a separate bowl, mix the flour, baking powder, and salt. Gradually incorporate the dry ingredients with the butter mixture.
4. Divide the dough in half and roll each into a 2-inch diameter cylinder.
5. Scatter the chopped pistachios on a plate. Roll each cookie dough log in the nuts and gently press them into the dough. Wrap them in plastic film and refrigerate for 2–3 hours.
6. Preheat the oven to 375°F. Using a sharp knife, slice the dough into ¼-inch rounds. Arrange them on ungreased cookie sheets. Press a whole pistachio into the center of each.
7. Bake for 7–9 minutes, until the edges are golden.

Apricot Balls

My grandmother kept her recipes in an empty chocolates box. On November 29, 1970, she wrote down this recipe from Alice Kennedy.

Makes 48 balls | Prep. time 30 min.

Ingredients
1 (1 ¼-pound) package dry apricots
1 cup sweetened condensed milk
2 cups sweetened shredded coconut (plus more for rolling)
½ cup white sugar

Directions

1. Finely chop the apricots. Mix in the sweetened condensed milk, coconut, and sugar.
2. Roll the mixture into 1-inch balls and roll them in additional coconut.

Jam Coconut Buttons

My grandmother's house has long been sold, but if I were to visit there even now, I might just check the bottom cupboard behind her chair. There was always a tin of these cookies in there, always. You just never know.

Makes 24 cookies | Prep. time 30 min. |
Cooking time 12–13 min. (per tray)

Ingredients
1 cup butter (at room temperature)
½ cup packed brown sugar
2 eggs, separated
1 teaspoon vanilla extract
2 ½ cups all-purpose flour
¼ teaspoon salt

1 ½ cups shredded coconut
¼ cup jelly or jam (your choice)

Directions
1. Preheat the oven to 375°F. Line two baking sheets with parchment.
2. In a medium bowl, beat the butter and sugar until fluffy. Add the egg yolks and vanilla and mix well. Mix in the flour and salt.
3. Lightly beat the egg whites in a bowl, and pour the coconut into a separate bowl.
4. Roll the cookie dough into 1-inch balls. One at a time, moisten them in the egg yolk and then roll them in the coconut. Set them 2 inches apart on the cookie sheets.
5. Using the tip of your finger or the handle of a spoon, make an indent in each cookie.
6. Measure half a teaspoon of jam into each indent.
7. Bake for 13–16 minutes, or until lightly browned.

Cinnamon Sugar Potato Doughnuts

This is an old New England recipe from the 1930s, excellent with a hot cup of tea. The texture is just beautiful as long as your potatoes are not too moist and heavy.

Serves 16 | Prep. time 20 min. | Cooking time 20 min.

Ingredients
¼ cup unsalted butter, softened
¾ cup sugar
1 large egg, room temperature
2 teaspoons vanilla extract
1 cup baked and riced Yukon Gold or russet potatoes
¼ cup buttermilk, at room temperature
2 cups all-purpose flour, plus more for dusting
1 teaspoon baking powder

1 teaspoon baking soda
½ teaspoon salt
¼ teaspoon ground nutmeg
Vegetable shortening for frying
Cinnamon sugar, for dusting (optional)

Directions

1. In a medium mixing bowl, combine the butter and sugar and beat until fluffy. Add the egg and vanilla and whisk until light and glossy.
2. Add the potato and buttermilk and mix until smooth.
3. Incorporate the flour, baking powder, baking soda, salt, and nutmeg and mix just until combined. The dough should be a little sticky; add a splash more milk if needed.
4. Heat the vegetable shortening for frying to a depth of 2–3 inches. (Oil can be used, but a crispier texture is achieved with shortening.)
5. Coat a clean surface generously with flour, and turn out the dough to flour both sides. Press it into a rectangle half an inch thick, and cut it into rounds with a doughnut cutter.
6. When the melted shortening is 375°F, cook the doughnuts in small batches, turning once. Take care not to let the oil cool too much.
7. Set the doughnuts on kitchen paper to drain, and toss with cinnamon sugar if desired.

SWEET LOAVES AND MUFFINS

Whole Wheat Bran Muffins

This is another recipe from my grandmother's box. My mother went through a "wheat bran" craze in the mid-1970s, and we ate many of these muffins!

Serves 12 | Prep. time 10 min. | Cooking time 15–17 min.

Ingredients

¼ cup oil

¼ cup sugar

¼ cup honey

2 eggs

1 cup milk

1 ½ cups wheat bran

1 cup whole wheat flour

1 ½ teaspoon baking powder

½ teaspoon baking soda

1 teaspoon salt

Directions

1. Preheat the oven to 400°F. Prepare a muffin tin with cooking spray or paper cups.
2. In a mixing bowl, combine the oil, sugar, honey, eggs, and milk.
3. Add the bran and mix well.
4. In a separate bowl, mix together the flour, baking powder, baking soda, and salt.
5. Stir the dry ingredients into the wet, and stir just to combine.
6. Spoon the batter into the prepared muffin cups and bake for 15–17 minutes.

Banana Rum Fruit Bread

Another entry from my grandmother's box: this one was a tiny clipping sandwiched in the folds of a knitting pattern for a toque. I couldn't resist giving it a try; it's a lovely cross between banana bread and fruitcake!

Serves 10 | Prep. time 15 min. | Soaking time 1 hour | Cooking time 1 hour.

Ingredients

¼ cup rum
1 cup mixed fruit peel and raisins
1 cup sugar
½ cup vegetable oil
2 eggs, lightly beaten
3 ripe bananas, mashed

1 teaspoon vanilla extract
2 cups all-purpose flour
1 teaspoon baking powder
½ teaspoon salt

Directions
1. Preheat the oven to 350°F. Butter a 9x5 loaf pan.
2. Combine the rum and fruit peel and let them sit for one hour.
3. Mix the sugar and oil until well combined. Add the eggs, mixing after each. Stir in the bananas and vanilla.
4. Add the flour, baking powder and salt, and mix just to combine. Fold in the rum and fruit mixture.
5. Pour the mixture into the loaf pan and bake for 1 hour, until a toothpick inserted in the center of the loaf comes out clean or with moist crumbs.

Old Fashioned Apple Loaf

This family recipe is moist and comforting, and the pecans give it a lovely texture.

Serves 10 | Prep. time 15 min. | Cooking time 45 min.

Ingredients
2 cups flour
2 teaspoons baking powder
¾ teaspoon cinnamon
Pinch ground nutmeg
¼ teaspoon salt
½ teaspoon baking soda
⅔ cup chunky applesauce
½ cup sugar
2 eggs

¼ cup oil
6 tablespoons milk
½ cup pecans, chopped

For the topping
2 tablespoons pecans, finely chopped
2 tablespoons margarine
1 tablespoon brown sugar

Directions
1. Preheat the oven to 350°F. Butter a 9x5 loaf pan.
2. Combine all the loaf ingredients and mix just to combine. Place them in the prepared loaf pan.
3. Combine the topping ingredients with a fork. Spread them in a line down the center of the loaf.
4. Bake for 45 minutes, or until a toothpick inserted in the center of the loaf comes out clean.

Spiced Pineapple Loaf

I wish I knew the original source of this recipe. It's moist and sweet with just the right balance of spice.

Serves 8 | Prep. time 20 min. | Cooking time 1 hour.

Ingredients
½ cup vegetable shortening
¾ cup sugar
2 eggs
1 ¾ cups all-purpose flour
2 teaspoons baking powder
½ teaspoon baking soda
½ teaspoon salt
1 teaspoon cinnamon
¼ teaspoon nutmeg

167

¼ teaspoon allspice

1 cup crushed pineapple with juices

Directions

1. Preheat the oven to 350°F. Butter a 9x5 loaf pan.
2. Cream the shortening and beat in the sugar and eggs.
3. In a separate bowl, whisk together the flour, baking powder, baking soda, salt, cinnamon, nutmeg, and allspice.
4. Gradually add the dry ingredients, alternately with the pineapple and juice, to the shortening mixture.
5. Spread the batter in the prepared loaf pan and bake for 1 hour. When a toothpick inserted in the center of the loaf comes out clean, or with a few moist crumbs, it's ready.
6. Cool the loaf completely before serving.

Old Fashioned Molasses Muffins

Molasses has fallen out of favor, which is a shame. These muffins are so good warm with a cold glass of milk—like a ginger cookie, but in muffin form.

Serves 12 | Prep. time 10 min. | Cooking time 18–20 min.

Ingredients

1 ¼ cups all-purpose flour
¼ cup sugar
½ teaspoon baking soda
½ teaspoon ground ginger
½ teaspoon cinnamon
¼ teaspoon nutmeg
¼ teaspoon salt

1 egg
½ cup water
¼ cup vegetable oil
¼ cup molasses

Directions

1. Preheat the oven to 350°F. Prepare a muffin tin with cooking spray or paper cups.
2. In a mixing bowl, combine the flour, sugar, baking soda, ginger, cinnamon, nutmeg, and salt.
3. In a separate bowl, beat the egg with the water, oil, and molasses.
4. Stir the wet ingredients into the dry, and stir just to combine.
5. Spoon the mixture into the muffin cups and bake for 18–20 minutes, until the top bounces back when pressed gently with a fingertip.

Cherry Coffee Cake Muffins

These vintage muffins are a little extra effort, but they're beautiful and delicious.

Serves 12 | Prep. time 10 min. | Cooking time 18–20 min.

Ingredients
1 ¼ cups flour
½ cup sugar
1 ½ teaspoons baking powder
¼ teaspoon salt
¼ cup cold butter
1 egg, lightly beaten

171

3 tablespoons milk

1 teaspoon vanilla

1 can cherry pie filling

For the topping
½ cup flour

¼ cup brown sugar

½ teaspoon cinnamon

¼ cup cold butter

Directions

1. Preheat the oven to 350°F. Prepare a muffin tin with cooking spray or paper cups.
2. Combine the flour, sugar, baking powder, and salt. Cut in the butter until coarse crumbs are formed.
3. In a separate bowl, combine the egg, milk, and vanilla. Beat them together and mix them into the dry ingredients.
4. Divine the batter into the muffin cups, and place a spoonful of cherry pie filling on top.
5. Make the topping. Mix the flour, brown sugar, and cinnamon. Cut in the butter.
6. Sprinkle the topping over the pie filling.
7. Bake for 18–20 minutes.

Orange Raisin Gems

These muffins hail from the 1940s. They're tart and sweet, and not quite like anything you'll find in a bakery today.

Serves 12 | Prep. time 10 min. | Cooking time 20 min.

Ingredients

2 cups sifted all-purpose flour
¾ teaspoon baking soda
½ teaspoon salt
⅓ cup sugar
½ cup raisins
1 egg, beaten
⅓ cup orange juice
1 teaspoon grated orange rind
⅔ cup buttermilk
⅓ cup shortening, melted

Directions

1. Preheat the oven to 425°F and prepare a muffin tin with butter or cooking spray.
2. Combine the flour, baking soda, salt, sugar, and raisins. Mix well, and set aside.
3. In a separate bowl, combine the egg, orange juice, orange rind, buttermilk, and melted shortening.
4. Add the dry ingredients and stir to moisten.
5. Fill the muffin cups two-thirds full and bake for 20 minutes.

RECIPE INDEX

ALSO BY LOUISE DAVIDSON

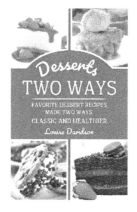

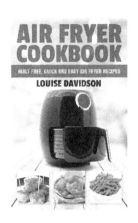

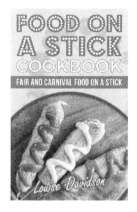

APPENDIX

Cooking Conversion Charts

1. Measuring Equivalent Chart

Type	Imperial	Imperial	Metric
Weight	1 dry ounce		28g
	1 pound	16 dry ounces	0.45 kg
Volume	1 teaspoon		5 ml
	1 dessert spoon	2 teaspoons	10 ml
	1 tablespoon	3 teaspoons	15 ml
	1 Australian tablespoon	4 teaspoons	20 ml
	1 fluid ounce	2 tablespoons	30 ml
	1 cup	16 tablespoons	240 ml
	1 cup	8 fluid ounces	240 ml
	1 pint	2 cups	470 ml
	1 quart	2 pints	0.95 l
	1 gallon	4 quarts	3.8 l
Length	1 inch		2.54 cm

* Numbers are rounded to the closest equivalent

2. Oven Temperature Equivalent Chart

Fahrenheit (°F)	Celsius (°C)	Gas Mark
220	100	
225	110	1/4
250	120	1/2
275	140	1
300	150	2
325	160	3
350	180	4
375	190	5
400	200	6
425	220	7
450	230	8
475	250	9
500	260	

* Celsius (°C) = T (°F)-32] * 5/9

** Fahrenheit (°F) = T (°C) * 9/5 + 32

*** Numbers are rounded to the closest equivalent

Image Credits

Introduction
By Pjrsoap [CC BY-SA 4.0 (https://creativecommons.org/licenses/by-sa/4.0)]

Old-Fashioned Buttermilk Pie
By Ralph Daily, CC BY 2.0, https://commons.wikimedia.org/w/index.php?curid=10358418

Jefferson Davis Pie
By Drmies - CC BY-SA 3.0, https://en.wikipedia.org/w/index.php?curid=48510510

Amish Applesauce Cake
By John Fladd from New Boston, NH, United States - Week 5 - Applesauce Cake on a Monkey Plate, CC BY-SA 2.0,

Molasses Stack Cake
By thebittenword.com - originally posted to Flickr as Apple Stack Cake, CC BY 2.0, https://commons.wikimedia.org/w/index.php?curid=6867630

Made in the USA
Las Vegas, NV
06 September 2022

54793229R00105